EASY PIANO

Rolling Stone ®

SHEET MUSIC ANTHOLOGY *of* ROCK & SOUL CLASSICS

25 SELECTIONS FROM THE

100 GREATEST SINGERS OF ALL TIME

Produced by
Alfred Music Publishing Co., Inc.
P.O. Box 10003
Van Nuys, CA 91410-0003
alfred.com

Printed in USA.

*No part of this book shall be reproduced, arranged, adapted, recorded, publicly performed, stored in a retrieval system,
or transmitted by any means without written permission from the publisher. In order to comply with copyright laws, please apply for
such written permission and/or license by contacting the publisher at alfred.com/permissions.*

ISBN-10: 0-7390-6526-2
ISBN-13: 978-0-7390-6526-6

 Contents printed on 100% recycled paper.

What Makes a Great Singer?
By Jonathan Lethem

There's something about a voice that's personal, not unlike the particular odor or shape of a given human body. Summoned through belly, hammered into form by the throat, given propulsion by bellows of lungs, teased into final form by tongue and lips, a vocal is a kind of audible kiss, a blurted confession, a soul-burp you really can't keep from issuing as you make your way through the material world. How helplessly candid! How appalling!

Contrary to anything you've heard, the ability to actually carry a tune is in no regard a disability in becoming a rock & roll singer, only a mild disadvantage. Conversely, nothing in the vocal limitations of a Lou Reed guarantees a "Pale Blue Eyes" every time out, any more than singing as crazy-clumsy as Tom Waits guarantees a "Downtown Train." Yet there's a certain time-tested sturdiness to the low-chops approach forged by touchstone figures like Bob Dylan and Jim Morrison and Jonathan Richman, one that helps define rock & roll singing.

For me, Bob Dylan and Patti Smith, just to mention two, are superb singers by any measure I could ever care about—expressivity, surprise, soul, grain, interpretive wit, angle of vision. Those two folks, a handful of others: their soul-burps are, for me, *the soul-burps of the gods*. The beauty of the singer's voice touches us in a place that's as personal as the place from which that voice has issued. If one of the weird things about singers is the ecstasy of surrender they inspire, another weird thing is the debunking response a singer can arouse once we've recovered our senses. It's as if they've fooled us into loving them, diddled our hard-wiring, located a vulnerability we thought we'd long ago armored over. Falling in love with a singer is like being a teenager every time it happens.

Singers *are* tricksters. Sometimes we'll wonder if they're more like movie actors than musicians per se—we'll decide that the "real" R.E.M. are embodied by Buck, Berry and Mills, not that kooky frontman Stipe, or the "real" Rolling Stones are Richards-Wood-Watts-Wyman, rather than that irritating capitalist Jagger. But beware—go down this route and soon you'll find yourself wondering how the Doors sound sans "Mr. Mojo Risin' " or imagining someone can better put across Dylan's gnarled syllables than Dylan himself. Firm evidence is on the table against both those lines of inquiry. In truth, so often what makes a band like the Stones or R.E.M. (or the band Dylan transformed from the Hawks into the Band) so truly unique and powerful is in how the instrumentalists rise to the challenge of creating a home for the vocalist's less-than-purely-musical approach to a song: the braggadocio or mumbling, the spoken asides or too many syllables crowded into a line that destroy traditional rhythm or measure, those movie-star flourishes that compel us to adore and resent the singer at once.

The funny thing about this kind of imposter anxiety is that it infects singers themselves, to the extent that certain well-known vocalists have been known to decorate themselves onstage with a carefully unplugged guitar (I know of a couple, but I'm not telling). And it certainly explains the "rockist" bias in favor of singers who are also the writers of the songs they sing. If a vocal performance that tenderizes our hearts is a kind of high-wire walk, an act breathtaking and preposterous at once, we can reassure ourselves that Neil Young or Gillian Welch or Joe Strummer have at least dug the foundations for the poles and strung the wire themselves. Singers reliant on existing or made-to-fit material, like Janis Joplin, Rod Stewart, Whitney Houston—or, for that matter, a band's pure vocal instrument, like Roger Daltrey—might just be birds alighting on someone else's wire. Listening to singers who are like magnificent animals wandering through a karaoke machine, we may derive a certain thrill from wondering if they find the same meaning in the lyrics they're putting across that the lyrics' writer intended, or any meaning at all—as opposed to dwelling in a realm of pure sound-as-emotion.

This points to what defines great singing in the rock-and-soul era: that some underlying tension exists in the space between singer and song. A bridge is being built across a void, and it's a bridge we're never sure the singer's going to manage to cross. The gulf may reside between vocal texture and the actual meaning of the words, or between the singer and band, musical genre, style of production or the audience's expectations. In any case, there's something beautifully uncomfortable at the root of the vocal style that defines the pop era. The simplest example comes at the moment of the style's inception, i.e. Elvis Presley: at first, listeners thought that the white guy was a black guy. It's not too much of an exaggeration to say that when Ed Sullivan's television show tossed this disjunction into everyone's living rooms, American culture was thrilled by it but also a little deranged, in ways we haven't gotten over yet. If few vocal styles since have had the same revolutionary potential, it wasn't for want of trying. When the Doors experimented with how rock & roll sounded fronted by sulky bombast, or the Ramones or Modern Lovers offered the sound of infantile twitching, a listener's first response may have been to regard their approaches as a joke. Yet that joke is the sound of something changing in the way a song can make us feel. In the cafe where I write this, Morrissey just came over the speakers, and it's pretty unmistakable that he came through the Doors Jim Morrison opened. Janis Joplin's voice howled in the wilderness for decades before Lucinda Williams came along to claim its tattered and glorious implications. In doing so, she deepened them.

Ultimately, the nature of the vocals in post-Elvis, post-Sam Cooke, post-Ray Charles popular music is the same as the role of the instrumental soloist in jazz. That's to say, if it isn't pushing against the boundaries of its form, at least slightly, it isn't doing anything at all. Whether putting across lines that happen to be written by the singer, or are instead concocted in a Brill Building or Motown-type laboratory, or covering a song pulled in from another genre, from the blues or bluegrass, or a show tune, the singer in rock, soul and pop has to be doing something ineffable that pulls against its given context. Etta James, Ray Davies, Mama Cass, Mark Kozelek, Levi Stubbs Jr.—these singers might not all seem like protest singers, but they are always singing *against* something; whether in themselves, in the band that's backing them, in the world they've been given to live in or the material they've been given to sing, or all at once. We judge pre-rock singing by how perfectly the lyric is served. That's the standard Frank Sinatra exemplifies. We judge popular vocals since 1956 by what the singer unearths that the song itself could never quite. It explains why voices such as Joan Baez or Emmylou Harris or Billy Joel never really seem to be singing in the contemporary idiom, no matter how much they roughen up their material or accompaniment, and why Elvis—or Dylan—is always rock, even singing "Blue Moon." It also explains precisely why such virtuosic pipes as Aretha Franklin's or, yes, Karen Carpenter's function in the new tradition. No lyric written by them or anyone else could ever express what their voices needed to, and they weren't going to wait for the instrumental solo, or for the flourish of strings, to put it across for them. They got it into their voice, and their voices got it out into the air, and from there it passed into our bodies. How can we possibly thank them enough?

CONTENTS

SINGER INDEX

The Greatest Singers of All Time
Excerpted from *Rolling Stone*® magazine's "The 100 Greatest Singers of All Time"

Mariah Carey

"When I was little," Mariah Carey says, "I used to wake up with a really raspy voice and"—she shifts to her signature squeak—"talk in a really high voice. My mother couldn't understand it, and she's an opera singer. But then I started to try to sing using that voice." Carey is famous for her staggering vocal range—including those ravishing high notes—and power. Her mastery of melisma, the fluttering strings of notes that decorate songs like "Vision of Love," inspired the entire *American Idol* vocal school, for better or worse, and virtually every other female R&B singer since the Nineties. But technical skill alone doesn't make for hits, and Carey's radiant, sweetly sexy presence has been knocking them out of the park for two decades. She's scored more Number One singles than any solo artist—18 and counting.

BORN: *March 27th, 1970*
KEY TRACKS: *"One Sweet Day," "Vision of Love," "Fantasy"*
INFLUENCED: *Brandy, Christina Aguilera, Leona Lewis*

ROLLING STONE® 100 GREATEST SINGERS RANK: »**No. 79**

MUSIC APPEARS ON PAGE 47: "Hero"

Ray Charles
By Billy Joel

Ray Charles had the most unique voice in popular music. He would do these improvisational things, a little laugh or a "Huh-hey!" It was as if something struck him as he was singing and he just had to react to it. He was getting a kick out of what he was doing. And his joy was infectious.

But there was something else I didn't realize until we sang together in the Eighties, on my song "Baby Grand." When he sings, he's not just singing soulfully. He is imparting his soul. You are hearing something deep within the man. I thought it would just turn me into this little nerd from Levittown, New York. But it didn't. It emboldened me. It was like an evangelical event. He was the minister and I was the congregation. I got all fired up.

Ray started out wanting to be Nat "King" Cole. When Nat went down low in a song, like "Mona Lisa," there was a growl in there that was kind of sexy. Ray took that to a whole other level. He took the growl and turned it into singing. He took the yelp, the whoop, the grunt, the groan, and made them music.

Also, he was a piano player. The piano is a percussion instrument. You put your body into it. Ray had a lot of unique body movements I didn't know until I saw him. Before I saw him, I heard those movements as he sang. I heard his shoulder go up a little on the left side, the way he lifted himself off the stool. Then I realized the voice I was hearing was also playing that piano.

The first Ray Charles I heard was *Modern Sounds in Country and Western Music*. He'd had hits before that, the R&B stuff, like "What'd I Say." But here is a black man giving you the whitest possible music in the blackest possible way, while all hell is breaking loose with the civil rights movement. When he sang "You Don't Know Me," I thought, "He isn't just singing the lyrics. He's saying, 'You don't know me. Get to know me.'"

He could be very sly with a song. His 1972 version of "America the Beautiful" is an iconic recording. There was so much feeling in his performance. It was his way of saying, "This is my country too. We gave you your popular music. This was ours before it was yours."

But Ray synthesized the blues into a language everybody could relate to. You can't listen to Ray Charles and not say, "This is a man who felt deeply, who has lived this music." He shows you his humanity. The spontaneity is evident. Another guy might say, "That was a mistake, we can't leave that in." No, Ray left it in. The mistake became the hook.

BORN: *September 23rd, 1930 (died June 10th, 2004)*
KEY TRACKS: *"What'd I Say, Pts. 1 & 2," "I Got a Woman," "You Don't Know Me," "Georgia on My Mind"*
INFLUENCED: *Van Morrison, Otis Redding, Stevie Wonder*

ROLLING STONE® 100 GREATEST SINGERS RANK: »**No. 2**

MUSIC APPEARS ON PAGE 112: "What'd I Say"

Sam Cooke
By Van Morrison

If a singer is not singing from the soul, I do not even want to listen to it—it's not for me.

Sam Cooke reached down deep with pure soul. He had the rare ability to do gospel the way it's supposed to be—he made it real, clean, direct. Gospel drove Sam Cooke through his greatest songs, the same way it did for Ray Charles, who came first, and Otis Redding.

He had an incomparable voice. Sam Cooke could sing anything and make it work. But when you're talking about his strength as a singer, range is not relevant. It was his power to deliver—it was about his phrasing, the totality of his singing.

He did a lot of great songs, but "Bring It on Home to Me" is a favorite. It's just a well-crafted song with a great lyric and melody. It's a song that's written to allow you to go wherever you can with it. "A Change Is Gonna Come" is another song I covered; it's a great arrangement.

Not many people can play this music anymore, not the way Sam Cooke did it, coming directly from the church. What can we learn from a singer like him, from listening to songs like "A Change Is Gonna Come"? It depends on who the singer is and what they are capable of, where their head is and how serious they are. But Sam Cooke was born to sing.

BORN: *January 22nd, 1931 (died December 11th, 1964)*
KEY TRACKS: *"A Change Is Gonna Come," "Bring It on Home to Me," "You Send Me"*
INFLUENCED: *Otis Redding, Art Garfunkel, Rod Stewart*

ROLLING STONE® 100 GREATEST SINGERS RANK: **》No. 4**

MUSIC APPEARS ON PAGE 116: "You Send Me"

Dion

Art Garfunkel describes Dion as "a bold extrovert of a singer," and Steve Van Zandt hears "the sneer of punk" in his late-Fifties and early-Sixties hits such as "The Wanderer" and "Runaround Sue." A key figure in doo-wop's transition to rock & roll, the Bronx-born singer defined an attitude of white-boy rebellion — and delivered his lyrics with a casual, swinging phrasing that rivals Sinatra. Heavyweights such as Elvis Presley, Bob Dylan, Bruce Springsteen and John Lennon were all on record as fans of his rowdy vocals. But Dion's favorite compliment came from an even more unimpeachable source. Once, at a television taping, Little Richard's mother, Leva Mae, took Dion aside and asked him, "You the boy that sings 'Ruby Baby'? Son, you got soul."

BORN: *July 18th, 1939*

KEY TRACKS: *"A Teenager in Love," "The Wanderer," "Runaround Sue," "Abraham, Martin and John"*

INFLUENCED: *Lou Reed, Paul Simon, Bruce Springsteen*

ROLLING STONE® 100 GREATEST SINGERS RANK: **》No. 63**

MUSIC APPEARS ON PAGE 82: "Runaround Sue"

Bob Dylan
By Bono

Bob Dylan did what very, very few singers ever do. He changed popular singing. And we have been living in a world shaped by Dylan's singing ever since. Almost no one sings like Elvis Presley anymore. Hundreds try to sing like Dylan. When Sam Cooke played Dylan for the young Bobby Womack, Womack said he didn't understand it. Cooke explained that from now on, it's not going to be about how pretty the voice is. It's going to be about believing that the voice is telling the truth.

To understand Bob Dylan's impact as a singer, you have to imagine a world without Tom Waits, Bruce Springsteen, Eddie Vedder, Kurt Cobain, Lucinda Williams or any other vocalist with a cracked voice, dirt-bowl yelp or bluesy street howl. It is a vast list, but so were the influences on Dylan, from the Talmudic chanting of Allen Ginsberg in "Howl" to the deadpan Woody Guthrie and Lefty Frizzell's murmur. There is certainly iron ore in there, and the bitter cold of Hibbing, Minnesota, blowing through that voice. It's like a knotted fist, and it allows Dylan to sing the most melancholy tunes and not succumb to sentimentality. What's interesting is that later, as he gets older, the fist opens up, to a vulnerability. I have heard him sing versions of "Idiot Wind" where he was definitely the idiot.

I first heard Bob Dylan's voice in the dark, when I was 13 years old, on my friend's record player. It was his greatest-hits album, the first one. The voice was at once modern, in all the things it was railing against, and very ancient. It felt strangely familiar to an Irishman. We thought America was full of superheroes, but it was a much humbler people in these songs—farmers, people who have had great injustices done to them. The really unusual thing about Bob Dylan was that, for a moment in the Sixties, he felt like the future. He was the Voice of a Generation, raised against the generation that came before. Then he became the voice of all the generations, the voices in the ground—these ghosts from the Thirties and the Dust Bowl, the romance of Gershwin and the music hall. For me, the pictures of him in his polka-dot shirt, the Afro and pointy shoes—that was a brief flash of lightning. His voice is usually put to the service of more ancient characters.

Here are some of the adjectives I have found myself using to describe that voice: howling, seducing, raging, indignant, jeering, imploring, begging, hectoring, confessing, keening, wailing, soothing, conversational, crooning. It is a voice like smoke, from cigar to incense, where it's full of wonder and worship. There is a voice for every Dylan you can meet, and the reason I'm never bored of Bob Dylan is because there are so many of them, all centered on the idea of pilgrimage. People forget that Bob Dylan had to warm up for Dr. King before he made his great "I have a dream" speech—the preacher preceded by the pilgrim. Dylan has tried out so many personas in his singing because it is the way he inhabits his subject matter. His closet won't close for all the shoes of the characters that walk through his stories.

I love that album *Shot of Love*. There's no production. You're in a room hearing him sing. And I like a lot of the songs that he worked on with Daniel Lanois—"Series of Dreams," "Most of the Time," "Dignity." That is the period where he moves me most. The voice becomes the words. There is no performing, just life—as Yeats says, when the dancer becomes the dance.

Dylan did with singing what Brando did with acting. He busted through the artifice to get to the art. Both of them tore down the prissy rules laid down by the schoolmarms of their craft, broke through the fourth wall, got in the audience's face and said, "I dare you to think I'm kidding."

BORN: *May 24th, 1941*

KEY TRACKS: *"Like a Rolling Stone," "Lay Lady Lay," "Visions of Johanna"*

INFLUENCED: *John Lennon, Bruce Springsteen, Patti Smith, Conor Oberst*

ROLLING STONE® 100 GREATEST SINGERS RANK: »**No. 7**

MUSIC APPEARS ON PAGE 57: "Like a Rolling Stone"

Art Garfunkel

"He is a pure and beautiful tenor voice, and there really is no one like him," says James Taylor about Art Garfunkel, whose singing blends lyricism with a remarkable ease of delivery. He brought sweetness and wonder to his classic harmonies with Paul Simon, a delicacy that defined those songs, and some of the hopes of the late Sixties. "I'm looking for controlled beauty," he says, a standard he learned as a child from the likes of Italian opera star Enrico Caruso. "Those arias—I love a song with a high, pole-vault peak." That describes solo hits such as 1973's "All I Know" and 1975's "I Only Have Eyes for You." "I like to sing heartfelt, where you address the mic with your honesty," says Garfunkel. "You try to be authentic as a person, with all the doubt, wonder, and mystery of being alive."

BORN: *November 5th, 1941*

KEY TRACKS: *"Bridge Over Troubled Water," "Scarborough Fair/Canticle" (Simon and Garfunkel), "All I Know" (solo)*

INFLUENCED: *Cat Stevens, James Taylor*

ROLLING STONE® 100 GREATEST SINGERS RANK: »**No. 86**

MUSIC APPEARS ON PAGE 22: "Bridge Over Troubled Water"

Levon Helm
By Jim James

There is something about Levon Helm's voice that is contained in all of our voices. It is ageless, timeless and has no race. He can sing with such depth and emotion, but he can also convey a good-old fun-time growl.

Since Papa Garth Hudson didn't really sing, I always felt that, vocally, Levon was the father figure in the Band. He always seems strong and confident, like a father calling you home, or sometimes scolding you. The beauty in Richard Manuel's singing was often the sense of pain and darkness he conveyed. Rick Danko had a lot of melancholy to his voice as well, but he could also be a little more goofy. They were all different shades of color in the crayon box, and Levon's voice is the equivalent of a sturdy old farmhouse that has stood for years in the fields, weathering all kinds of change yet remaining unmovable.

The best thing about Levon is that he has so many sides, from the sound his voice gave to the Band's rich harmonies to how he can rip it up on songs like "Yazoo Street Scandal," "Don't Ya Tell Henry," "Up on Cripple Creek" and "Rag Mama Rag." He can pop in for sensitive moments, such as in between Manuel's vocals in "Whispering Pines." And he laid down one of the greatest recorded pop vocal performances of all time: "The Weight." I was fortunate to get to go to one of his Midnight Rambles a few years back when My Morning Jacket were recording up in the Catskills. To see him walk out on that stage and sit down behind the drum kit in person was a thrill. No one else plays the drums or sings like Levon, much less doing it at the same time.

There is a sense of deep country and family in Levon's voice, a spirit that was there even before him, deep in the blood of all singers who have heard him, whether they know it or not.

BORN: *May 26th, 1940*

KEY TRACKS: *"The Weight," "The Night They Drove Old Dixie Down"*

INFLUENCED: *Jeff Tweedy, Lucinda Williams, John Hiatt*

ROLLING STONE® 100 GREATEST SINGERS RANK: ≫**No. 91**

MUSIC APPEARS ON PAGE 109: *"The Weight"*

Whitney Houston

The daughter of R&B and gospel singer Cissy Houston, Whitney grew up around family friends Aretha Franklin and Gladys Knight; Dionne Warwick was a cousin. "When I started singing," she once said, "it was almost like speaking." By the time she was 22, Whitney had emerged as the greatest female voice of her generation: Her 1985 debut alone included the monster hits "Saving All My Love for You," "How Will I Know" and "The Greatest Love of All." Her voice is a mammoth, coruscating cry: Few vocalists could get away with opening a song with 45 unaccompanied seconds of singing, but Houston's powerhouse version of Dolly Parton's "I Will Always Love You" is a tour de force.

BORN: *August 9th, 1963*

KEY TRACKS: *"The Greatest Love of All," "I Wanna Dance with Somebody," "Saving All My Love for You," I Will Always Love You"*

INFLUENCED: *Beyoncé, Mariah Carey, Faith Evans, Mary J. Blige*

ROLLING STONE® 100 GREATEST SINGERS RANK: ≫**No. 34**

MUSIC APPEARS ON PAGE 42: *"The Greatest Love of All"*

Michael Jackson
By Patrick Stump of Fall Out Boy

Michael Jackson is a perfect storm of innate talent and training. His singing as a child is astounding: He just nailed "I Want You Back"—there's maybe one bum note on that song, which is crazy to me, because he was only 11 years old.

One of the key elements of his style is how he uses his voice as an instrument. His signature grunts—"ugh," "ah" and all that—are rhythmic things that guitar players or drummers usually do. He's one of the most rhythmic singers ever—Prince emulated James Brown a lot more, but Michael Jackson approximated it more naturally.

And he has insane range. I can sing pretty high, but I had to drop "Beat It" a half step when I sang it. He sings this incredibly high note—I think it's a high C or even a high C-sharp, which no one can hit—on "Beat It," as well as "Billie Jean" and "Thriller." What people don't realize is that he can go pretty deep too. You hear that on "Burn This Disco Out," on *Off the Wall*—he goes deep into his range, which blows me away.

When somebody gets as big as he did, you lose sight of how avant-garde and revolutionary they are, but Michael Jackson pushed the boundaries of pop and R&B. Think about it: On "Beat It," you had an R&B singer doing a full-on rock song with Eddie Van Halen. Or the intro on "Man in the Mirror": He's got this reverb in his voice, and any time he goes "uh!" it goes for miles. To me, that's up there with some Brian Eno shit. That's how far out there it is.

BORN: *August 29th, 1958 (died June 25th, 2009)*

KEY TRACKS: *"I Want You Back" (the Jackson 5), "Billie Jean," "Man in the Mirror" (solo)*

INFLUENCED: *Justin Timberlake, Chris Brown, Usher*

ROLLING STONE® 100 GREATEST SINGERS RANK: ≫**No. 25**

MUSIC APPEARS ON PAGE 26: *"Billie Jean"*

Mick Jagger
By Lenny Kravitz

I sometimes talk to people who sing perfectly in a technical sense who don't understand Mick Jagger. But what he does is so complex: His sense of pitch and melody is really sophisticated. His vocals are stunning, flawless in their own kind of perfection. There are certain songs where he just becomes a different person. Take "Angie": I've never heard that tone from him since, and it wasn't there before. And I love when he sings falsetto, like on "Emotional Rescue" or "Fool to Cry."

I like him best when he's singing super-raw. When I co-produced "God Gave Me Everything" (for *Goddess in the Doorway*), he did what he thought would be a scratch vocal. He barely knew the lyric—he was reading off a piece of paper. There were no stops, just one take. Bam! It ended up being the vocal we used on the record.

Mick is a disciplined artist, completely dedicated to his craft. His voice has changed somewhat and has a different texture, but it's stronger now. One time the Stones were on tour, and during a two-week break Mick and I went on vacation in the Bahamas. We'd hang out during the day, go to the beach, shop at the market, cook dinner, drink wine. In the evening he would go to the bottom floor of the place where we were staying and put on a Rolling Stones soundcheck tape—just the band playing songs without him singing. He would stay down there, dancing and singing to keep himself in shape. Your voice is like a muscle. If you're on the road and you stop for two weeks and then go back to do a show, you're going to get hoarse. So he was down there every night practicing. As a result, at 65 years of age, he's stronger than ever.

The beauty of that experience was sitting in a living room hearing "Brown Sugar" and "Satisfaction" live through the floor. That was my entertainment every night. It was very surreal.

BORN: *July 26th, 1943*
KEY TRACKS: *"Gimme Shelter," "Sympathy for the Devil," "Satisfaction"*
INFLUENCED: *Jack White, Steven Tyler, Iggy Pop*
ROLLING STONE® 100 GREATEST SINGERS RANK: ⟩⟩**No. 16**

MUSIC APPEARS ON PAGES 86: "(I Can't Get No) Satisfaction"

Etta James

"There's a lot going on in Etta James' voice," says Bonnie Raitt. "A lot of pain, a lot of life, but, most of all, a lot of strength." James is often thought of as the ultimate blues mama, her voice a steamroller fueled by brass and sass. But as the lush, soaring "At Last," a Number Two R&B hit in 1961, reveals every time it's played as first dance at a wedding, James—still going strong in her sixth decade of performing despite a notoriously hard-knock life—isn't limited to wailing: she's equally as powerful and entirely distinctive whether she's singing pop, jazz, ballads, or rock. "She can be so rauchous and down one song, and then break your heart with her subtlety and finesse the next," says Raitt. "As raw as Etta is, there's a great intelligence and wisdom in her singing."

BORN: *January 25th, 1938*
KEY TRACKS: *"At Last," "A Sunday Kind of Love," "Tell Mama"*
INFLUENCED: *Janis Joplin, Bonnie Raitt, Christina Aguilera*
ROLLING STONE® 100 GREATEST SINGERS RANK: ⟩⟩**No. 22**

MUSIC APPEARS ON PAGE 14: "At Last"

Elton John

John Lennon once told *Rolling Stone* that when he heard Elton John singing "Your Song"—the 1970 breakthrough ballad that spotlighted John's voice and its union of rock & roll grandness with deep soul feeling—he thought, "Great, that's the first new thing that's happened since we happened." Only a few years earlier, John had claimed, "I can't really sing." Once he found his voice, though, he quickly turned out to have a dumbfounding stylistic range, unleashing his singsong falsetto and his ferocious hard-rock bellow. "He was mixing his falsetto and his chest voice to really fantastic effect in the Seventies," says Ben Folds. "There's that point in 'Goodbye Yellow Brick Road,' where he sings, 'on the *grooound*'—his voice is all over the shop. It's like jumping off a diving board when he did that."

BORN: *March 25th, 1947*
KEY TRACKS: *"Your Song," "Goodbye Yellow Brick Road," "Tiny Dancer"*
INFLUENCED: *Rivers Cuomo, George Michael, Axl Rose*
ROLLING STONE® 100 GREATEST SINGERS RANK: ⟩⟩**No. 38**

MUSIC APPEARS ON PAGE 104: "Tiny Dancer"

Janis Joplin

"She was shaking that shake that she did, and was screaming. I'd never seen anything like it," says Melissa Etheridge of seeing Janis Joplin on *The Ed Sullivan Show* back in 1969. Joplin's gravelly rasp, over the psychedelic blues of Big Brother and the Holding Company (on 1968's breakthrough *Cheap Thrills*), and the rough-hewn country soul on her later solo albums, represented an entirely different approach for female vocalists: wild and uninhibited yet still focused and deliberate. Her performances were more about passionate abandon and nuanced phrasing than perfect pitch. "She would just kinda sing and scream and cry," says Etheridge, "and she'd sound like an old black woman—which is exactly what she was trying to sound like."

BORN: *January 19th, 1943 (died October 4th, 1970)*

KEY TRACKS: *"Piece of My Heart," "Cry Baby," "Me and Bobby McGee"*

INFLUENCED: *Bonnie Raitt, Sheryl Crow, Lucinda Williams*

ROLLING STONE® 100 GREATEST SINGERS RANK: ⟫**No. 28**

MUSIC APPEARS ON PAGES 70: "Piece of My Heart"

Jerry Lee Lewis

Few artists have attacked singing with the ferocity of Jerry Lee Lewis, a key combustible element in the rock & roll Big Bang of the Fifties. Just as he percussively hammered the keyboard of his piano, the Killer could transform his voice exclusively into a rhythm instrument, often tearing at his lyrics until the words become staccato nonsense syllables and he sounds like one of the faithful speaking in tongues. "It was evangelical," Steve Van Zandt says of Lewis' singing. Lewis moved effortlessly from shouting rockabilly to pure, classic country, scoring eight Number One hits on the country-singles chart. "He mystifies me, he's so good," says Art Garfunkel. "He's having a great time. He's rhythmically united with the piano, and the groove is sublime. He leaves you speechless."

BORN: *September 29th, 1935*

KEY TRACKS: *"Great Balls of Fire," "Whole Lotta Shakin' Goin' On," "Breathless"*

INFLUENCED: *Elton John, Kid Rock, John Fogerty*

ROLLING STONE® 100 GREATEST SINGERS RANK: ⟫**No. 67**

MUSIC APPEARS ON PAGE 39: "Great Balls of Fire"

Joni Mitchell

Joni Mitchell began as the archetype of the folkie female singer-songwriter, an heir to Joan Baez. But she quickly moved forward, incorporating influences from jazz and the blues. "Joni Mitchell heard Billie Holiday sing 'Solitude' when she was about nine years old—and she hasn't been the same since," says Herbie Hancock. Those lessons of emotional vulnerability are evident in her delicate soprano trill, as well as in the undisguised wear of the sultry voice of her later work, punctuated by her jazzy syncopation. "Joni's got a strange sense of rhythm that's all her own," Bob Dylan told *Rolling Stone*. Above all, Mitchell won't be boxed in. "The way she phrases always serves the lyrics perfectly, and yet her phrasing can be different every time," Hancock says. "She's a fighter for freedom."

BORN: *November 7th, 1943*

KEY TRACKS: *"Both Sides Now," "Help Me," "Raised on Robbery"*

INFLUENCED: *Robert Plant, Jewel, Fiona Apple*

ROLLING STONE® 100 GREATEST SINGERS RANK: ⟫**No. 42**

MUSIC APPEARS ON PAGE 17: "Big Yellow Taxi"

Van Morrison

John Lee Hooker called Van Morrison "my favorite white blues singer." Morrison has left his mark on over 40 years' worth of rock, blues, folk, jazz and soul, as well as several genres that only really exist on his records. He's the most painterly of vocalists, a master of unexpected phrasing whose voice can transform lyrics into something abstract and mystical—most famously on his repetition of "...and the love that loves the love...," on "Madame George," from *Astral Weeks*. Morrison's growls and ululations inspired singers from Bob Seger to Bruce Springsteen to Dave Matthews. Sometimes they can even be an overwhelming influence: Bono said that he had to stop listening to Morrison's records before making U2's *The Unforgettable Fire* because "I didn't want his very original soul voice to overpower my own."

BORN: *August 31st, 1945*

KEY TRACKS: *"Brown Eyed Girl," "Moondance," "Tupelo Honey"*

INFLUENCED: *Elvis Costello, Bono, Bruce Springsteen, Ray LaMontagne*

ROLLING STONE® 100 GREATEST SINGERS RANK: ⟫**No. 24**

MUSIC APPEARS ON PAGE 62: "Moondance"

Steve Perry

"Other than Robert Plant, there's no singer in rock that even came close to Steve Perry," says *American Idol* judge Randy Jackson, who played bass with Perry in Journey. "The power, the range, the tone—he created his own style. He mixed a little Motown, a little Everly Brothers, a little Zeppelin." When he was 10 years old, Perry heard Sam Cooke's "Cupid" on his mom's car radio, and decided he had to be a singer. After singing in a college choir, he joined Journey at the age of 28, quickly revealing a penchant for quavering, reverb-soaked melodrama that appealed to millions of fans—but few rock critics. Yet his technical skills (those high notes!), pure tone and passionate sincerity now seem undeniable. "He lives for it and loves it," says Jackson. "I just saw him not long ago, and he still has the golden voice."

BORN: *January 22nd, 1949*

KEY TRACKS: *"Oh Sherrie," "Don't Stop Believin'," "Open Arms"*

INFLUENCED: *Chris Daughtry, Chad Kroeger, Rob Thomas*

ROLLING STONE® 100 GREATEST SINGERS RANK: »**No. 76**

MUSIC APPEARS ON PAGE 36: "Don't Stop Believin'"

Wilson Pickett

"When Wilson Pickett screamed, he screamed notes," producer Jerry Wexler once said. "His voice was powerful, like a buzz saw, but it wasn't ever out of control. It was always melodic." Pickett's signature shout served as the climax for many of his 38 hit singles. "You can feel it comin'," said Pickett, "and you don't let go until the moment is exactly right." The man known as "the Wicked Pickett" and the "Midnight Mover" was soul's purest badass: Immortal songs like 1965's "In the Midnight Hour" and 1966's "Mustang Sally" brought a new level of ferociousness to R&B belting. But Pickett's good friend Solomon Burke notes that Pickett had another side. "Wilson was able to hold that note until you felt it," says Burke. "He made you listen."

BORN: *March 18th, 1941 (died January 19th, 2006)*

KEY TRACKS: *"In the Midnight Hour," "Land of 1,000 Dances," "Mustang Sally"*

INFLUENCED: *Bob Seger, Bruce Springsteen, Joe Cocker*

ROLLING STONE® 100 GREATEST SINGERS RANK: »**No. 68**

MUSIC APPEARS ON PAGE 66: "Mustang Sally"

Robert Plant

As a teenager in the English Midlands, Robert Plant was obsessed with the rawest American blues. "When I saw Sleepy John Estes and heard that voice—part pain, part otherworldly—I went, 'I want that voice,'" Plant told *Rolling Stone* in 2006. Somehow, he got that voice, and more: The unearthly howl he unleashed with Led Zeppelin was a bluesman crossed with a Viking deity. Singing like a girl never seemed so masculine, and countless hard-rock singers would shred their vocal cords reaching for the notes Plant gained by birthright. "His voice is picturesque," says collaborator Alison Krauss. "It sounds so new and so old at the same time, with this crazy European mystery to it."

BORN: *August 20th, 1948*

KEY TRACKS: *"Dazed and Confused," "Immigrant Song," "Sea of Love"*

INFLUENCED: *David Lee Roth, Freddie Mercury, Axl Rose*

ROLLING STONE® 100 GREATEST SINGERS RANK: »**No. 15**

MUSIC APPEARS ON PAGE 77: "Stairway to Heaven"

Axl Rose

"Axl sings the most beautiful melodies with the most aggressive tones and the most outrageous, freakish range," says Sebastian Bach. "There's maybe five people in the world that can sing in his range." Slash once described the sound of Rose's voice in slightly different terms: It's like "the sound that a tape player makes when the cassette finally dies and the tape gets ripped out," he said, "but in tune." It's immediately identifiable, with a combination of brute force and subtlety that is easy to overlook amid the sonic assault of Guns N' Roses. Ballads like "Patience" and "November Rain" reveal a startling intimacy, even vulnerability, but it's his fearsome screech on full-throttle metal like "Welcome to the Jungle" that can still peel paint off the walls, more than 20 years later.

BORN: *February 6th, 1962*

KEY TRACKS: *"Sweet Child O' Mine," "Paradise City," "November Rain"*

INFLUENCED: *Josh Todd (Buckcherry), Sebastian Bach*

ROLLING STONE® 100 GREATEST SINGERS RANK: »**No. 64**

MUSIC APPEARS ON PAGE 90: "Sweet Child O' Mine"

Dusty Springfield

"What makes a great singer is that you have to be completely naked within a song," says Shelby Lynne, who recently released an album of Dusty Springfield covers. "Dusty was open to being fragile and letting her guard down." A conservatively raised English girl, Springfield was a folk singer until she discovered R&B after hearing the Exciters' "Tell Him" while walking along a New York street. Songs like "I Only Want to Be with You" combined intelligence and energy. Her tendency to linger a shade behind the beat on ballads lent her soul singing a wonderful languor, but when she belted, she could rattle the windows. "Her voice wasn't black and it wasn't white," says Darlene Love, whom Springfield greatly admired. "It was totally unique. You knew it was Dusty when she came on the radio."

BORN: *April 16th, 1939 (died March 2nd, 1999)*
KEY TRACKS: *"I Only Want to Be With You," "Son of a Preacher Man"*
INFLUENCED: *Duffy, Amy Winehouse*

ROLLING STONE® 100 GREATEST SINGERS RANK: **≫No. 35**

MUSIC APPEARS ON PAGE 54: "I Only Want to Be with You"

Bruce Springsteen

"When Bruce Springsteen does those wordless wails, like at the end of 'Jungleland,' that's the definition of rock & roll to me," says Melissa Etheridge. "He uses his whole body when he sings, and he puts out this enormous amount of force and emotion and passion." Springsteen has used numerous vocal approaches over the past four decades: soul shouting, Roy Orbison belting, Elvis-style crooning, country-folk drawling, garage-rock hollering. "He finds the emotional drama in the characters of his songs," says Etheridge. "When he sings 'The River,' he's going to break your heart." When Bono inducted Springsteen into the Rock & Roll Hall of Fame in 1999, he said Springsteen's voice sounded as "if Van Morrison could ride a Harley-Davidson."

BORN: *September 23rd, 1949*
KEY TRACKS: *"Thunder Road," "Born in the U.S.A.," "Girls in Their Summer Clothes"*
INFLUENCED: *Eddie Vedder, Jon Bon Jovi, Brandon Flowers, Win Butler*

ROLLING STONE® 100 GREATEST SINGERS RANK: **≫No. 36**

MUSIC APPEARS ON PAGE 95: "Thunder Road"

Tina Turner

"I'll never forget the first time I saw (Tina) perform," said Beyoncé. "I never in my life saw a woman so powerful, so fearless." Turner started touring with the Ike and Tina Turner Revue almost half a century ago; her breakthrough was their blazing 1971 cover of Creedence Clearwater Revival's "Proud Mary," which included the declaration that she never does anything "nice and easy." "She was so direct, so raw," says John Fogerty, who wrote the song. Age has only deepened the ache and grit in her powerhouse cries and moans during her long career as a solo artist. Melissa Etheridge said that Turner's voice defies classification. "You can't say soul, R&B, rock & roll," Etheridge said. "She's all of it! She can squeeze passion from any line."

BORN: *November 26th, 1939*
KEY TRACKS: *"Proud Mary," "River Deep—Mountain High," "What's Love Got to Do with It"*
INFLUENCED: *Beyoncé, Mick Jagger, Mary J. Blige*

ROLLING STONE® 100 GREATEST SINGERS RANK: **≫No. 17**

MUSIC APPEARS ON PAGE 74: "Proud Mary"

Steven Tyler

Steven Tyler has a theory about how singing first began. "It had to be with the first primate uttering a moan during sex," he says. "I truly believe that's where the passion of voice comes from." Every line Tyler sings is informed by a leer and a wink, whether overtly ("Love in an Elevator") or with more subtlety ("Walk This Way"). In the course of nearly four decades fronting Aerosmith, Tyler has defined both the sound and style of the lead singer in a hard-rock band. "It's hard to separate the singer from the person," says Aerosmith guitarist Joe Perry. "You need personality to be a frontman." Tyler has that in spades, along with—amid all the yelps, groans, growls and squeals—an unerring sense of pitch. "As Tony Bennett said, 'Without heart, this is no art,'" Tyler says. "I wear my heart on my sleeve."

BORN: *March 26th, 1948*
KEY TRACKS: *"Sweet Emotion," "Dream On," "Walk This Way"*
INFLUENCED: *David Lee Roth, Axl Rose, Scott Weiland*

ROLLING STONE® 100 GREATEST SINGERS RANK: **≫No. 99**

MUSIC APPEARS ON PAGE 50: "I Don't Want to Miss a Thing"

Luther Vandross

No singer made the Top 40 sound so intimate—often painfully so—as Luther Vandross. "Singing allows me to express all the mysteries hidden inside," he once said. Vandross grew up worshiping at the altar of Aretha Franklin, Dionne Warwick and Diana Ross, then labored throughout the Seventies singing everything from Burger King commercials to sessions with David Bowie (on *Young Americans*), before emerging as the dominant R&B vocalist of his era. His warm, rich singing on hits like "Never Too Much" defined soul during the years between disco and hip-hop, influencing a generation of vocalists — including Mariah Carey, who was petrified to duet with Vandross on a cover of "Endless Love" in 1994. "It was intimidating to stand next to him," she says. "Luther was incomparable—his voice was velvety, smooth, airy, with an unmistakable tone."

BORN: *April 20th, 1951 (died July 1st, 2005)*
KEY TRACKS: *"Never Too Much," "Superstar," "A House Is Not a Home"*
INFLUENCED: *Alicia Keys, John Legend*

ROLLING STONE® 100 GREATEST SINGERS RANK: »**No. 54**

MUSIC APPEARS ON PAGE 31: "Dance with My Father"

AT LAST

Music by Harry Warren
Lyrics by Mack Gordon
Arranged by Dan Coates

BIG YELLOW TAXI

Words and Music by Joni Mitchell
Arranged by Dan Coates

Brightly

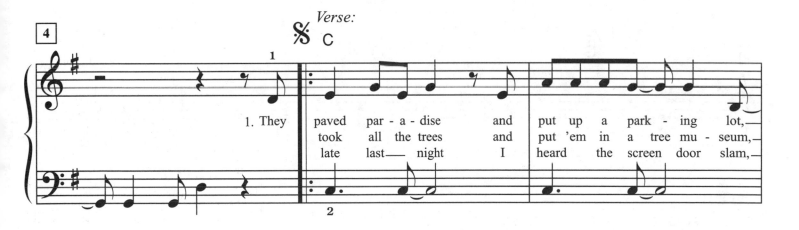

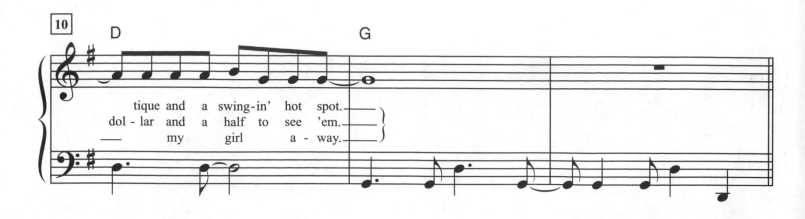

tique and a swing-in' hot spot.
dol - lar and a half to see 'em.
___ my girl a - way.

Chorus:

Don't it al - ways seem___ to go that you don't know what you got___

___ till it's gone. They paved par - a - dise and put up a park - ing

lot. ___ Ooh,___ bop bop.___ Ooh,___ bop___ bop bop.___ 2. They

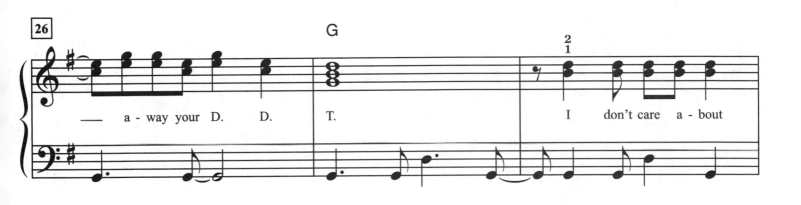

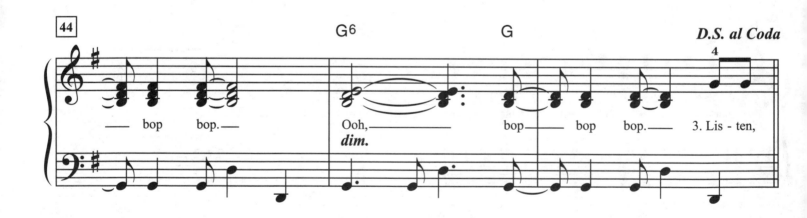

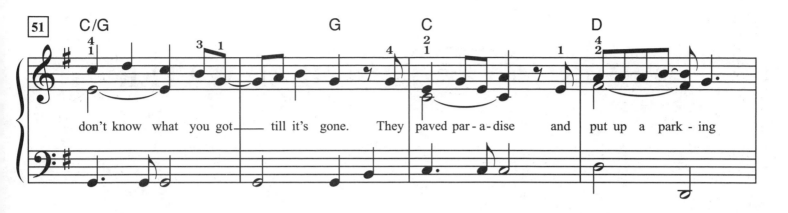

don't know what you got___ till it's gone. They paved par - a - dise ___ and put up a park - ing

lot.___ Hey, ___ hey, hey.___ They paved par - a - dise ___ to put up a park - ing

lot.___ Ooh,___ bop bop.___ They paved par - a - dise ___ and put up a park - ing

lot.___

BRIDGE OVER TROUBLED WATER

Words and Music by Paul Simon
Arranged by Dan Coates

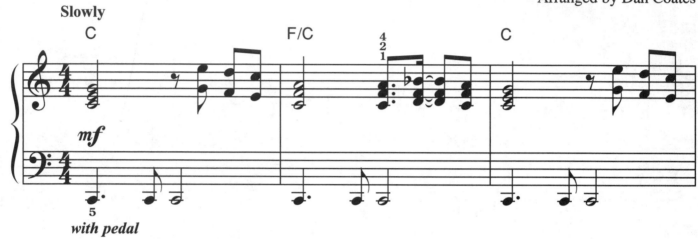

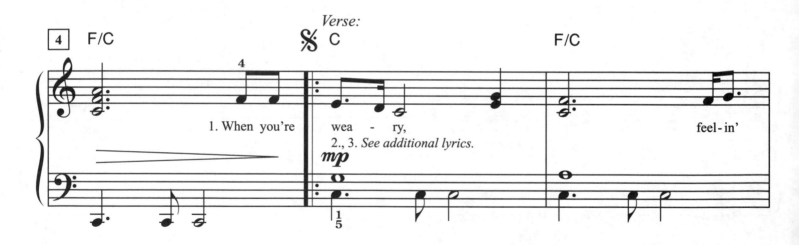

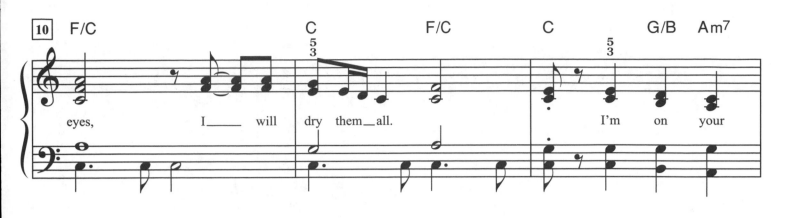

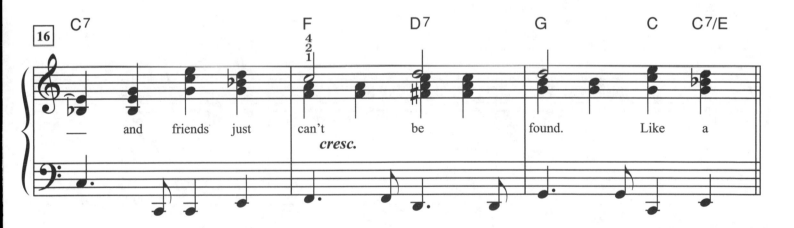

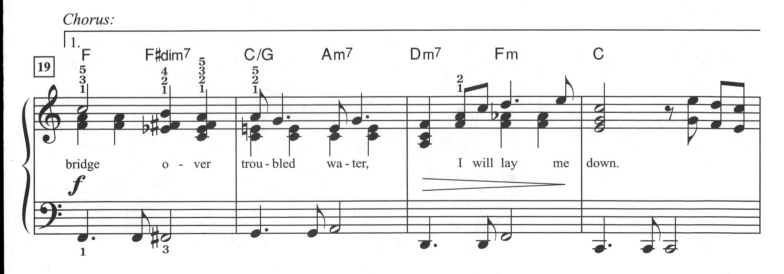

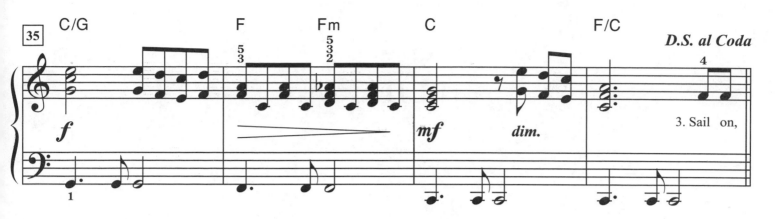

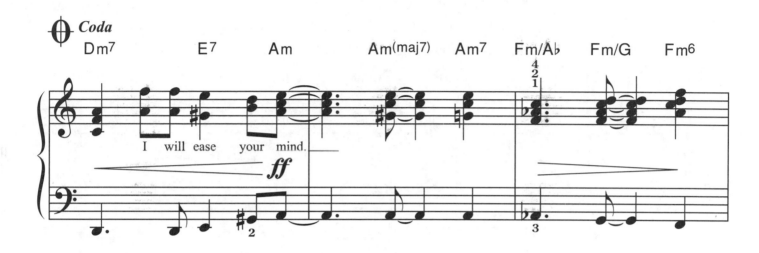

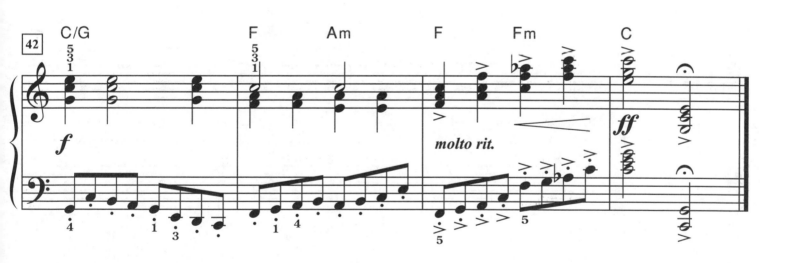

Verse 2:
When you're down and out,
When you're on the street,
When evening falls so hard, I will comfort you.
I'll take your part when darkness comes
And pain is all around.
Like a bridge over troubled water, I will lay me down.
Like a bridge over troubled water, I will lay me down.

Verse 3:
Sail on, silver girl, sail on by.
Your time has come to shine,
All your dreams are on their way.
See how they shine, if you need a friend.
I'm sailing right behind.
Like a bridge over troubled water, I will ease your mind.
Like a bridge over troubled water, I will ease your mind.

BILLIE JEAN

Written and Composed by Michael Jackson
Arranged by Dan Coates

Moderately, with a steady rock beat

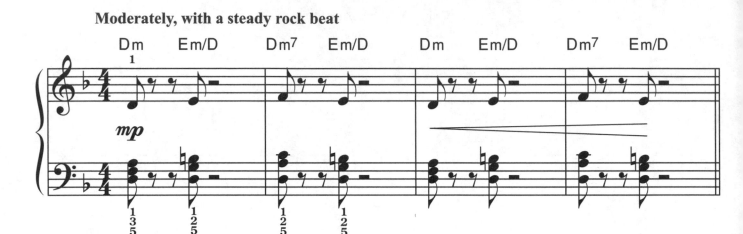

Verse:

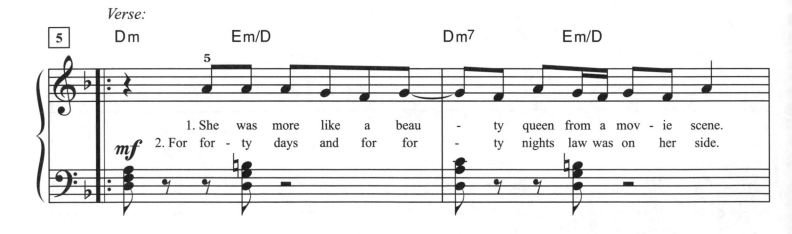

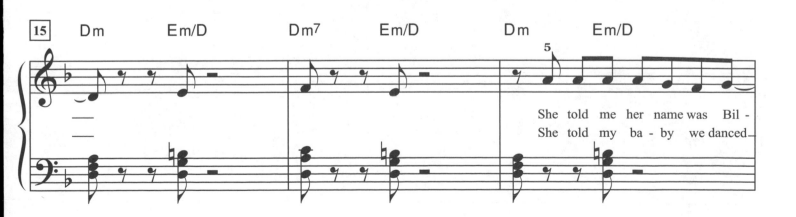

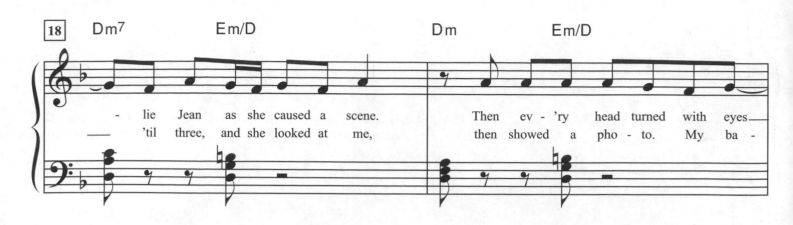

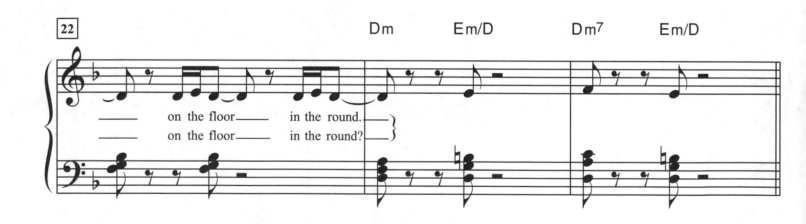

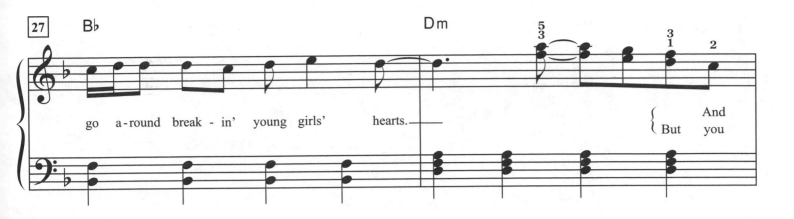

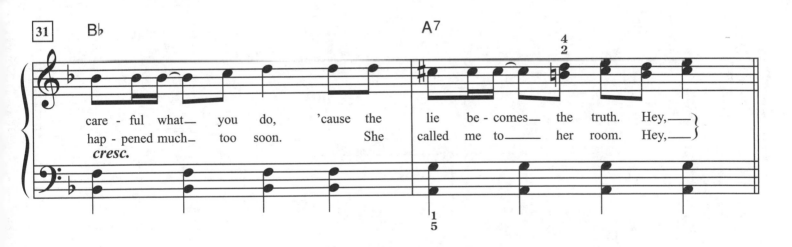

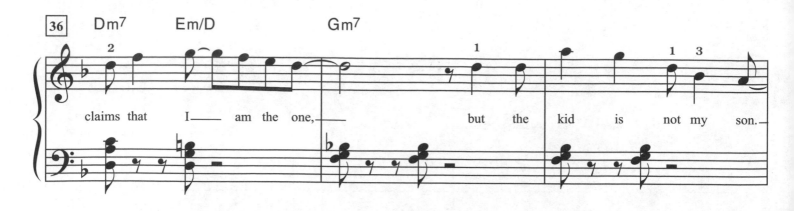

claims that I___ am the one,___ but the kid is not my son.

___ She says I___ am the one,___ but the

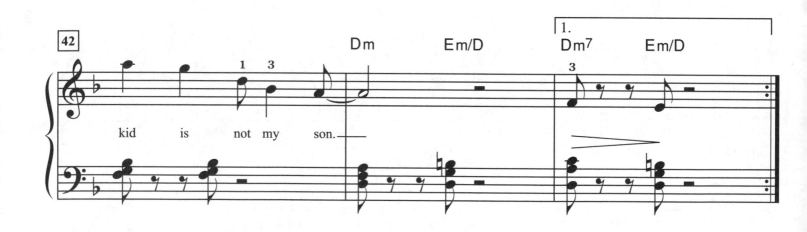

kid is not my son.___

DANCE WITH MY FATHER

Words and Music by
Richard Marx and Luther Vandross
Arranged by Dan Coates

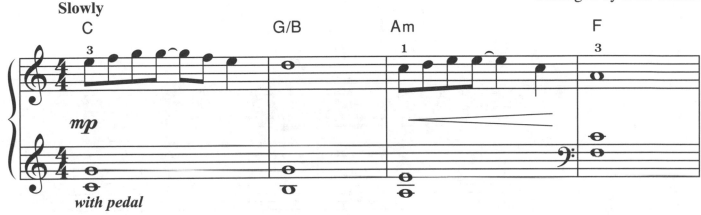

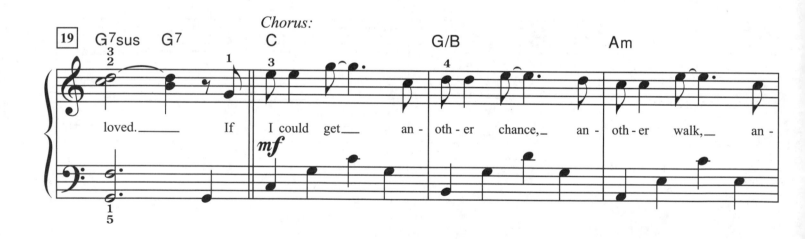

love,___ love___ to dance with my fa - ther a - gain.

2. When gain.

Some - times, I'd lis - ten out - side___ her door, and I'd hear how my moth - er cried___

___ for him. I pray for her e - ven more___ than me. I pray for her e - ven more___

34

Ev - 'ry night I fall a - sleep, and this is all I ev - er dream.

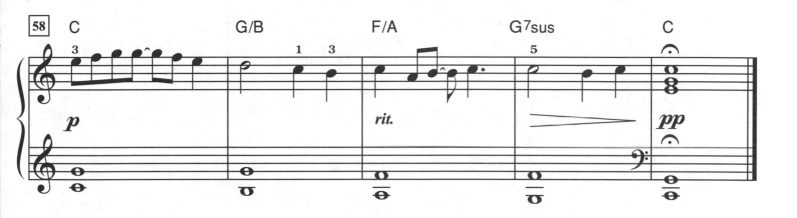

Verse 2:
When I and my mother would disagree,
To get my way, I would run from her to him.
He'd make me laugh just to comfort me,
Then finally make me do just what my mama said.
Later that night, when I was asleep,
He'd left a dollar under my sheet.
Never dreamed that would be gone from me.

Chorus 2:
If I could steal one final glance,
One final step,
One final dance with him,
I'd play a song that would never, ever end.
'Cause I'd love, love, love
To dance with my father again.

DON'T STOP BELIEVIN'

Words and Music by
Jonathan Cain, Neal Schon and Steve Perry
Arranged by Dan Coates

38

Verse 3:
A singer in a smoky room,
The smell of wine and cheap perfume.
For a smile they can share the night
It goes on and on and on and on.

Verse 4:
Working hard to get my fill.
Everybody wants a thrill,
Payin' anything to roll the dice
Just one more time.

Verse 5:
Some will win and some will lose,
Some were born to sing the blues.
Oh, the movie never ends,
It goes on and on and on and on.

GREAT BALLS OF FIRE

Words and Music by
Otis Blackwell And Jack Hammer
Arranged by Dan Coates

Brightly, with a rock beat

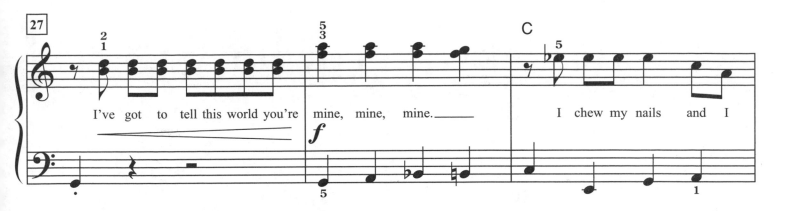

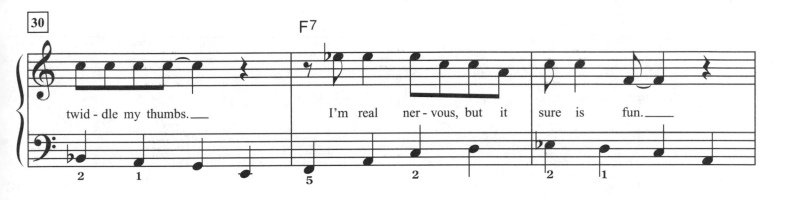

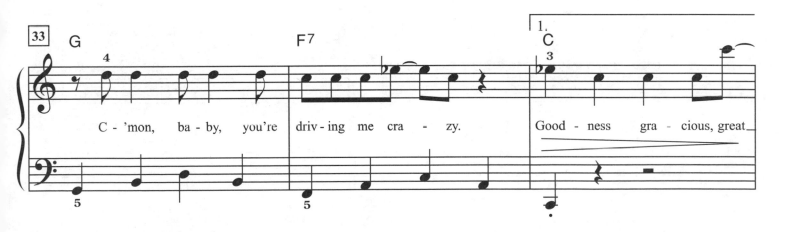

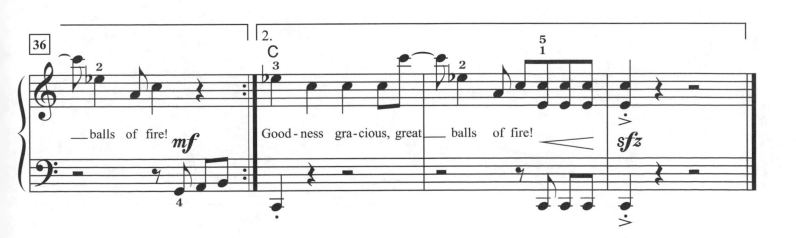

THE GREATEST LOVE OF ALL

Words by Linda Creed
Music by Michael Masser
Arranged by Dan Coates

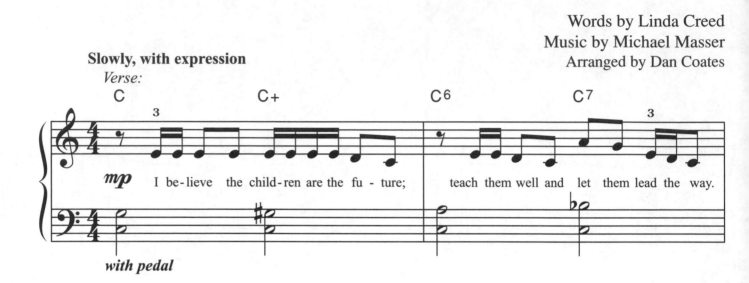

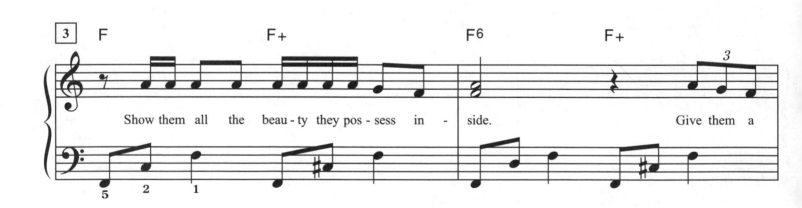

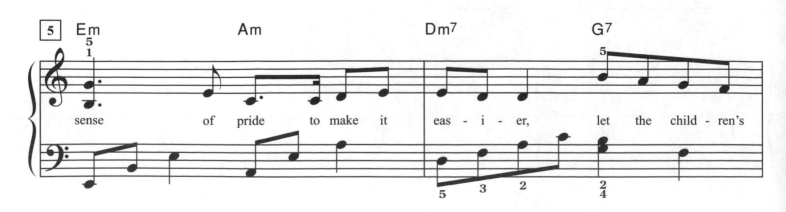

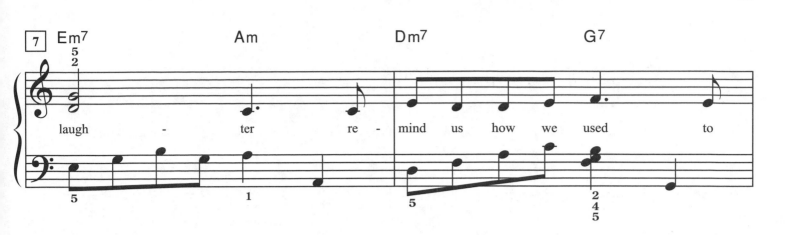

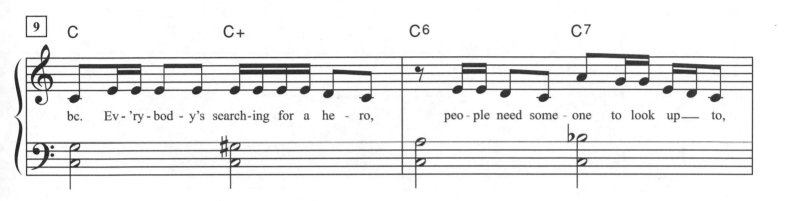

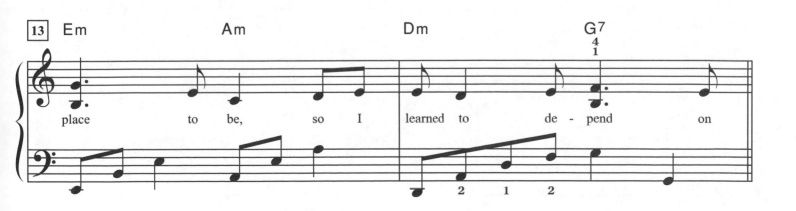

44

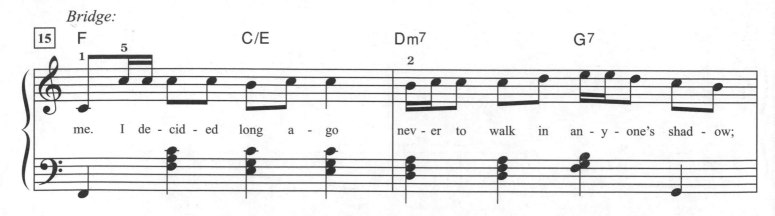

Bridge:

15 | F | C/E | Dm7 | G7

me. I de - cid - ed long a - go nev - er to walk in an - y - one's shad - ow;

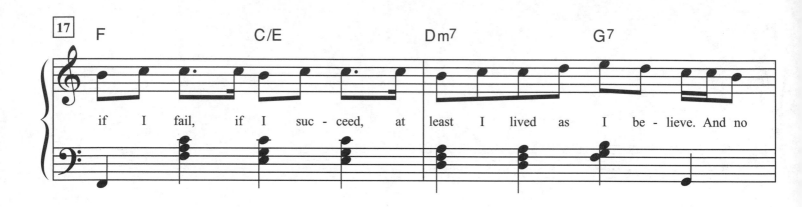

17 | F | C/E | Dm7 | G7

if I fail, if I suc - ceed, at least I lived as I be - lieve. And no

19 | F | C/E | Dm7 | G7

mat - ter what they take from me, they can't take a - way my dig - ni - ty. Be - cause the

cresc.

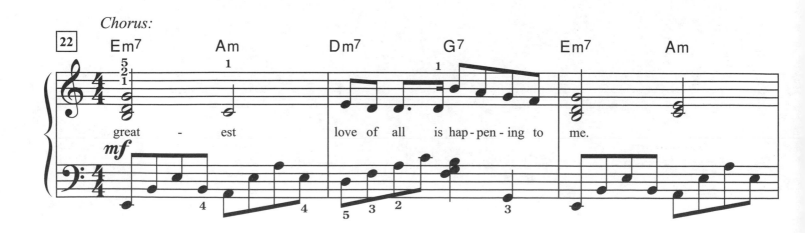

Chorus:

22 | Em7 | Am | Dm7 | G7 | Em7 | Am

great - est love of all is hap - pen - ing to me.

mf

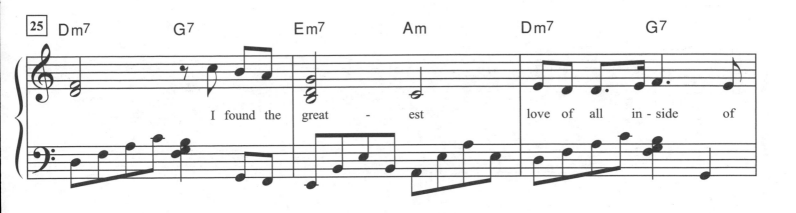

I found the great - est love of all in - side of

me. The great - est love of all

is eas - y to a - chieve.

Learn - ing to love your - self is the great - est love of

dim.

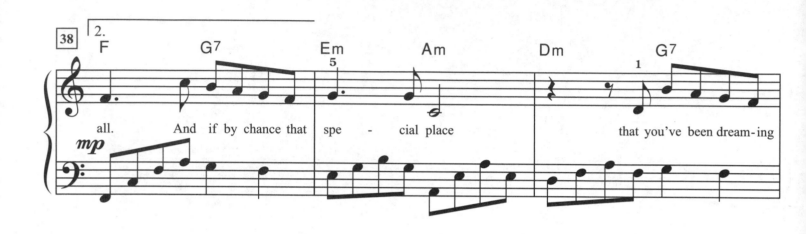

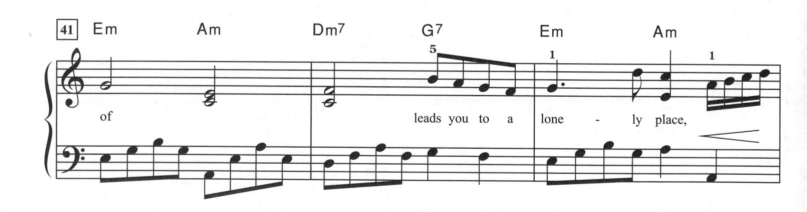

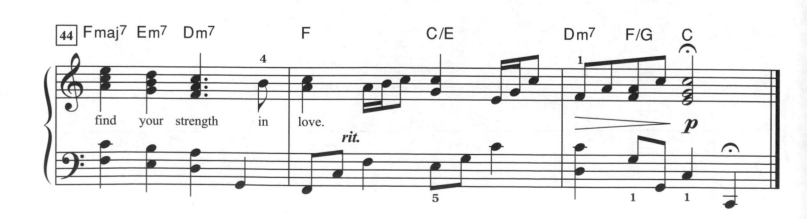

HERO

Words and Music by
Walter Afanasieff And Mariah Carey
Arranged by Dan Coates

I DON'T WANT TO MISS A THING

Words and Music by Diane Warren
Arranged by Dan Coates

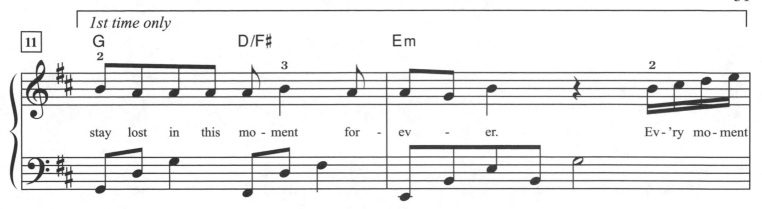

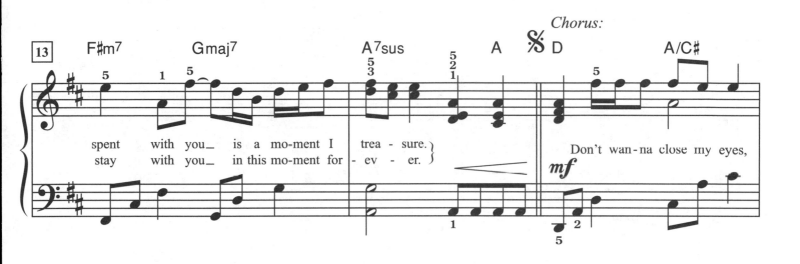

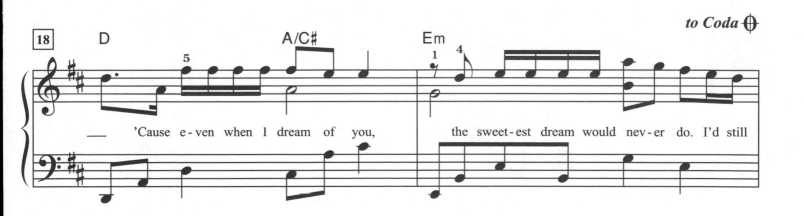

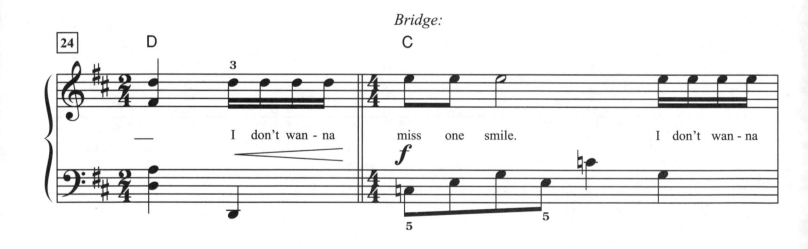

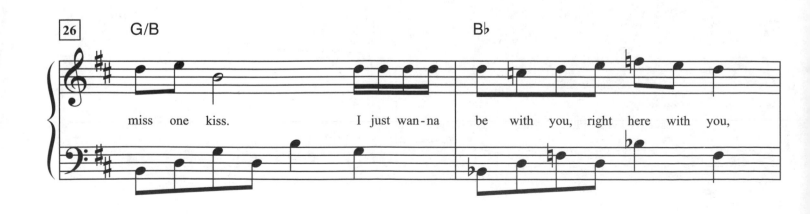

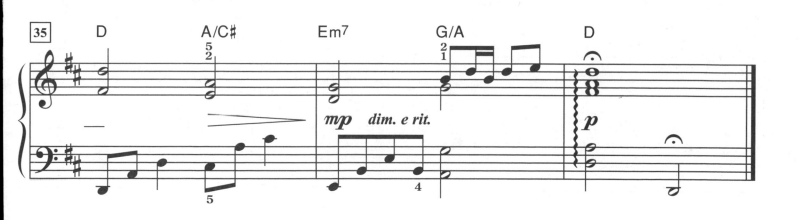

I ONLY WANT TO BE WITH YOU

Words and Music by
Mike Hawker and Ivor Raymonde
Arranged by Dan Coates

Bright dance tempo

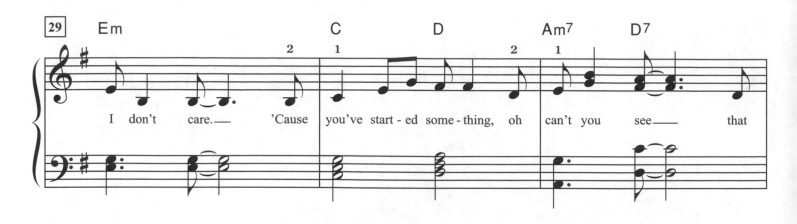

29 Em — C — D — Am7 — D7

I don't care.— 'Cause you've start-ed some-thing, oh can't you see—— that

32 G — Em — Am7 G C C#dim D

ev - er since we met you've had a hold on me?— No mat - ter what you do,—

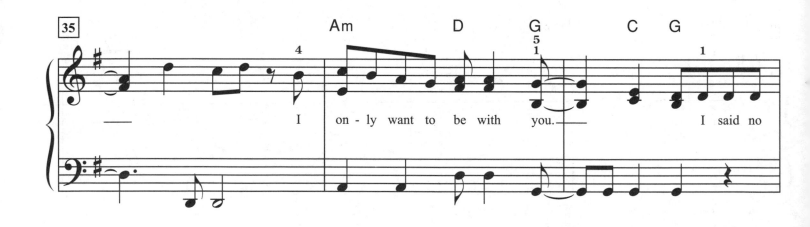

35 — Am D G C G

I on - ly want to be with you.— I said no

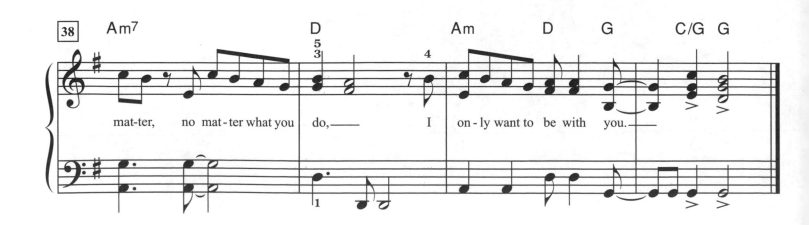

38 Am7 — D — Am D G C/G G

mat-ter, no mat-ter what you do,— I on - ly want to be with you.—

LIKE A ROLLING STONE

Words and Music by Bob Dylan
Arranged by Dan Coates

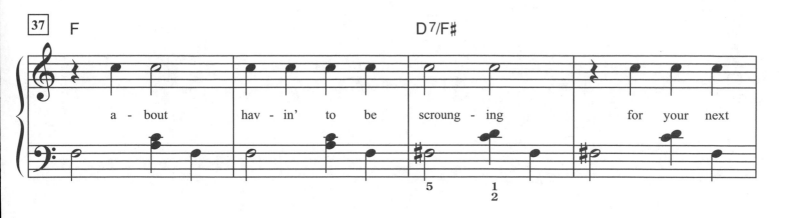

a - bout hav - in' to be scroung - ing for your next

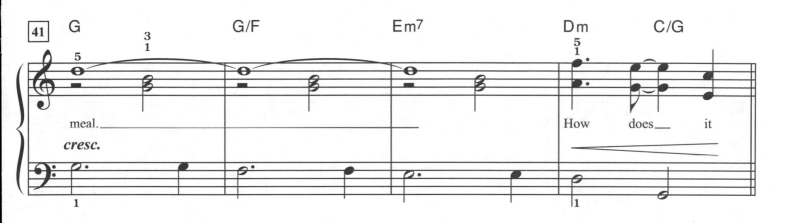

meal._____ How does__ it

cresc.

Chorus:

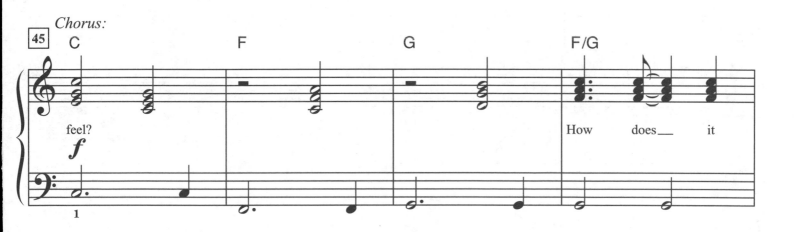

feel? How does__ it

f

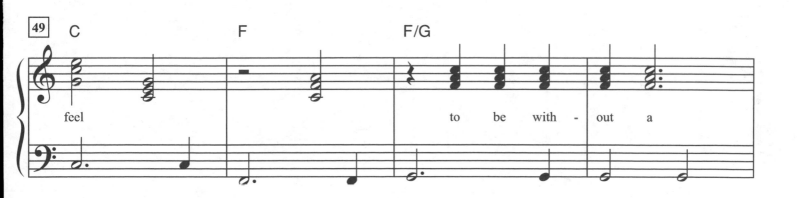

feel to be with - out a

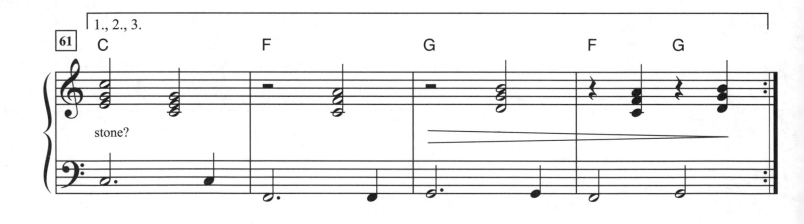

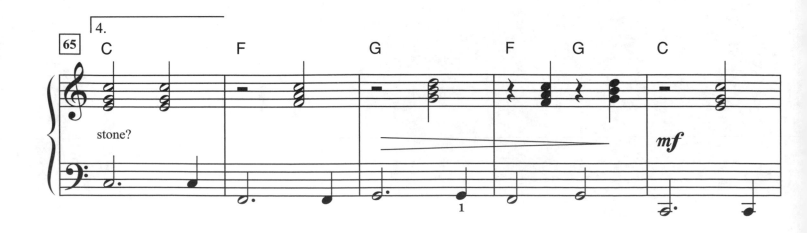

Verse 2:
Oh, you've gone to the finest school, alright, Miss Lonely,
But you know you only used to get juiced in it.
Nobody's ever taught you how to live out on the street
And now you're gonna have to get used to it.
You say you never compromise
With the mystery tramp, but now you realize
He's not selling any alibis
As you stare into the vacuum of his eyes
And say, "Do you want to make a deal?"
(To Chorus:)

Verse 3:
Oh, you never turned around to see the frowns on the jugglers and the clowns
When they all did tricks for you?
Never understood that it ain't no good,
You shouldn't let other people get your kicks for you.
You used to ride on a chrome horse with your diplomat
Who carried on his shoulder a Siamese cat.
Ain't it hard when you discovered that
He really wasn't where it's at
After he took from you everything he could steal?
(To Chorus:)

Verse 4:
Princess on the steeple and all the pretty people,
They're all drinkin', thinkin' that they got it made.
Exchanging all precious gifts,
But you better take your diamond ring,
You'd better pawn it, babe.
You used to be so amused
At Napoleon in rags and the language that he used.
Go to him now, he calls you, you can't refuse.
When you got nothin', you got nothin' to lose.
You're invisible now, you got no secrets to conceal.
(To Chorus:)

MOONDANCE

Words and Music by Van Morrison
Arranged by Dan Coates

skies. And all the leaves on the trees are fall - ing to the
run. And when you come, my heart will be wait - ing to make

sound of the breez-es that blow. And I'm try - ing to please___ to the call -
sure that you're nev-er a - lone. There and then all my dreams___ will come true,___

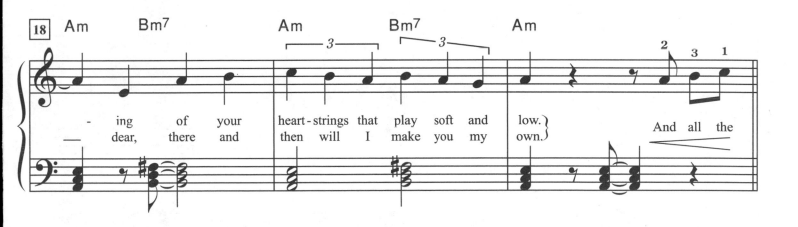

- ing of your heart-strings that play soft and low.} And all the
___ dear, there and then will I make you my own.}

Chorus:

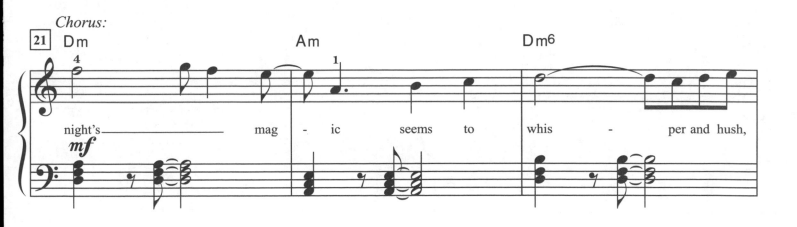

night's___ mag - ic seems to whis - per and hush,

mf

MUSTANG SALLY

Words and Music by Bonny Rice
Arranged by Dan Coates

Moderate rhythm and blues

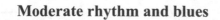

Verse:

Sal - ly, now, ba - by,   guess you bet-ter slow___ your Mus - tang

down.___   You been

run-nin' all o - ver town,___ ___ now,___   oh, I guess I have to put your flat feet on the

ground.___

One of these ear - ly morn - ings, I'm gon-na be wip-in' your__ weep-in'

eyes.

eyes.

Verse 2:
I bought you a brand new Mustang,
'Bout Nineteen sixty-five.
Now you come around, signifying a woman,
You don't wanna let me ride.
Mustang Sally, now, baby,
Guess you better slow that Mustang down.
You been runnin' all over town,
Oh, I've got to put your flat feet on the ground.
(To Chorus:)

PIECE OF MY HEART

Words and Music by
Jerry Ragovoy and Bert Russell
Arranged by Dan Coates

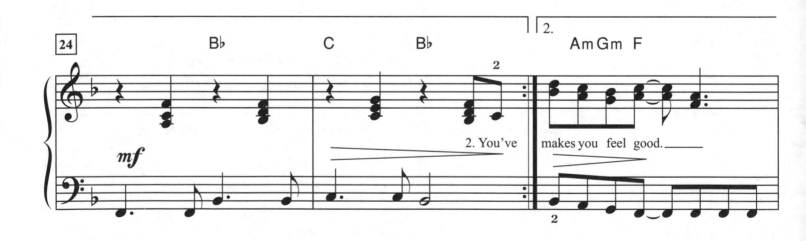

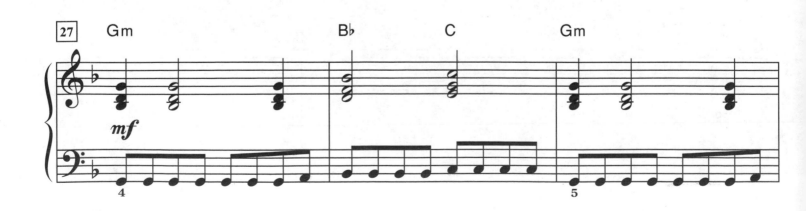

Verse 2:
You're out on the streets lookin' good,
And, baby, deep down in your heart
I guess you know that it ain't right.
Never, never, never, never, never,
Never hear me when I cry at night,
Baby, I cry all the time.
But each time I tell myself that I,
Well, I can't stand the pain.
But when you hold me in your arms,
I'll sing it once again.
I said come on, come on, come on, come on and...
(To Chorus:)

PROUD MARY

Words and Music by John C. Fogerty
Arranged by Dan Coates

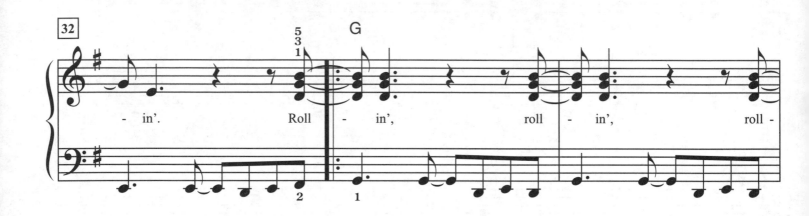

STAIRWAY TO HEAVEN

Words and Music by
Jimmy Page and Robert Plant
Arranged by Dan Coates

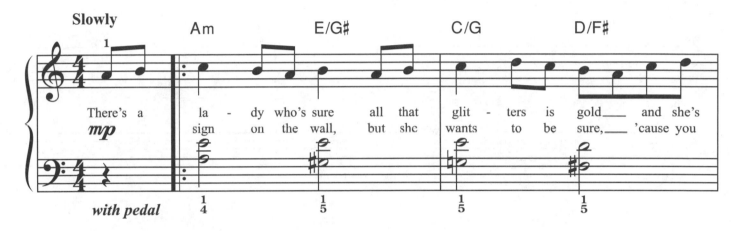

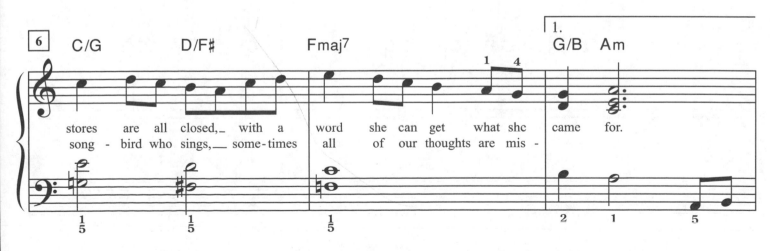

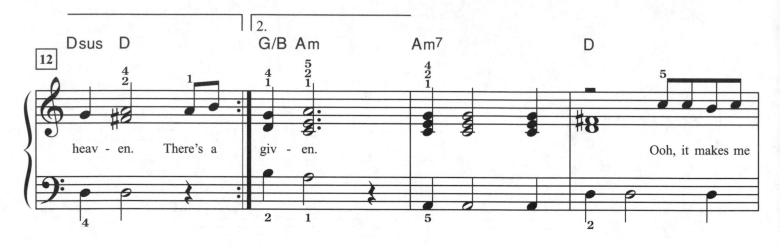

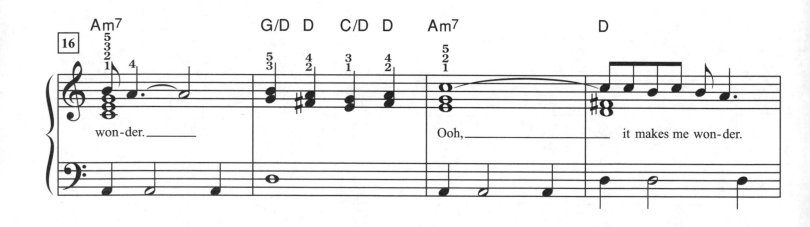

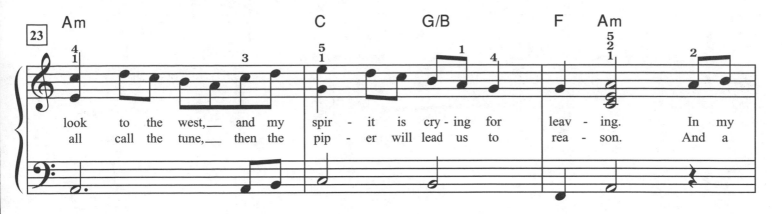

look to the west,___ and my spir - it is cry - ing for leav - ing. In my
all call the tune,___ then the pip - er will lead us to rea - son. And a

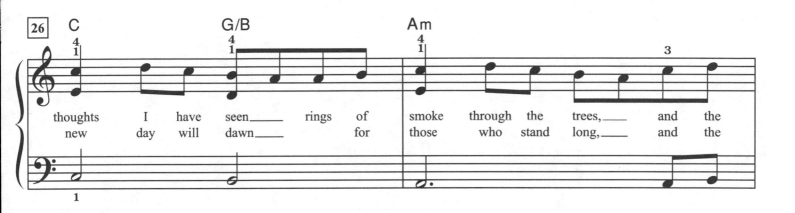

thoughts I have seen___ rings of smoke through the trees,___ and the
new day will dawn___ for those who stand long,___ and the

voic - es of those who stand look - ing. And it's laugh - ter.
for - ests will ech - o with

With a strong beat

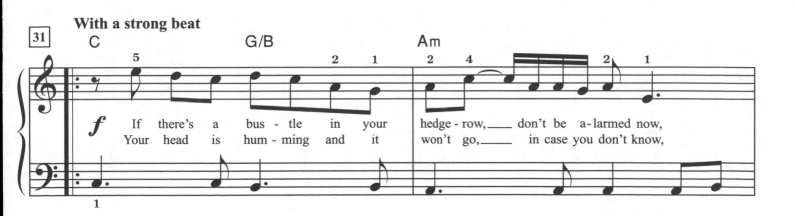

If there's a bus - tle in your hedge - row,___ don't be a-larmed now,
Your head is hum - ming and it won't go,___ in case you don't know,

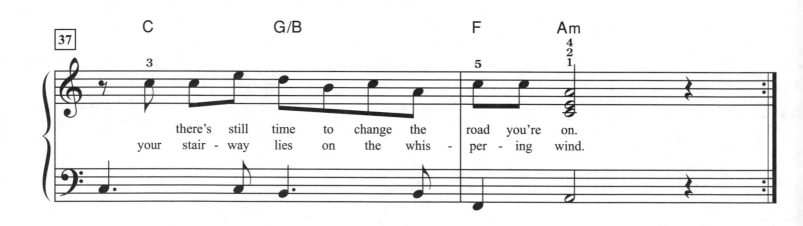

soul.___
hard,___

There walks a la - dy we all know,___
the tune will come to you at last,___

who shines white light and wants to show___
when all are one and one is all,___

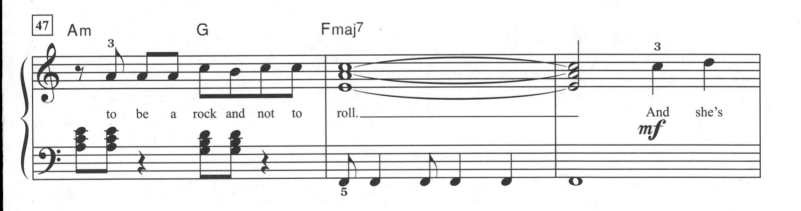

to be a rock and not to roll.___ And she's

buy - ing a stair - way to heav - en.___

RUNAROUND SUE

Words and Music by
Dion Di Mucci and Ernest Maresca
Arranged by Dan Coates

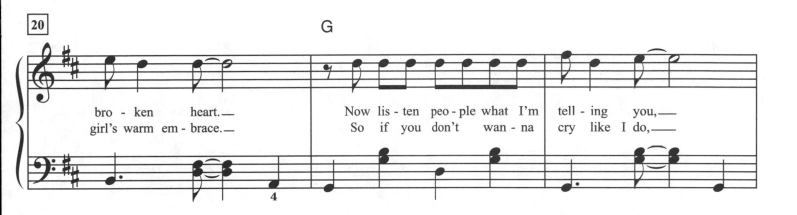

1. I should have known it from the ver - y start,— this girl will leave you with a
2. I miss her lips and the smile on her face,— the touch of her hair and this

bro - ken heart.— Now lis - ten peo - ple what I'm tell - ing you,—
girl's warm em - brace.— So if you don't wan - na cry like I do,——

a - keep a - way from a - Run - a - round Sue. Oh, oh,——

oh, oh,—— oh, oh.——

She likes to trav-el a - round, she'll

love you but she'll put you down. Now peo - ple let me put you wise,

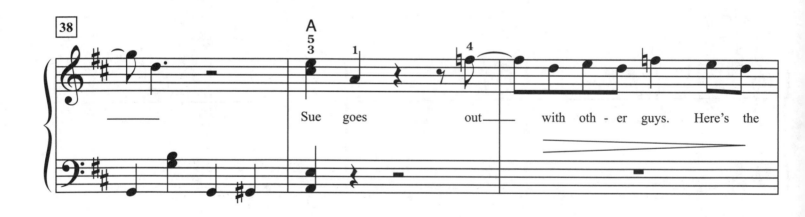

Sue goes out with oth - er guys. Here's the

mor - al of the sto - ry from the guy who knows, I fell in love and my love

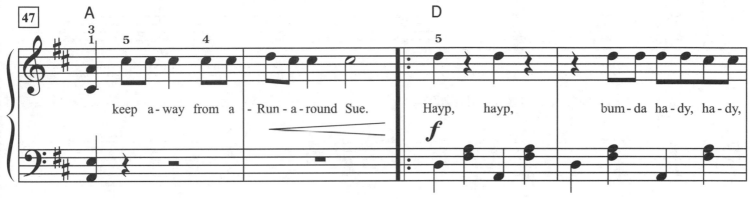

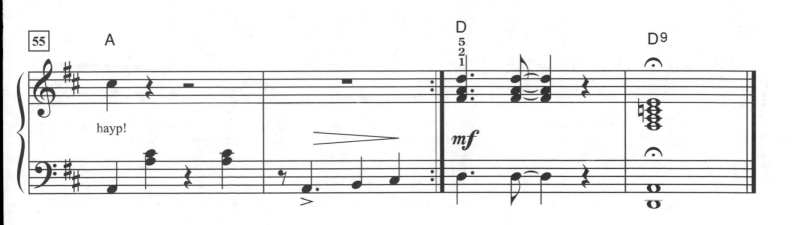

(I CAN'T GET NO) SATISFACTION

Words and Music by
Mick Jagger and Keith Richards
Arranged by Dan Coates

Moderately, with a steady rock beat

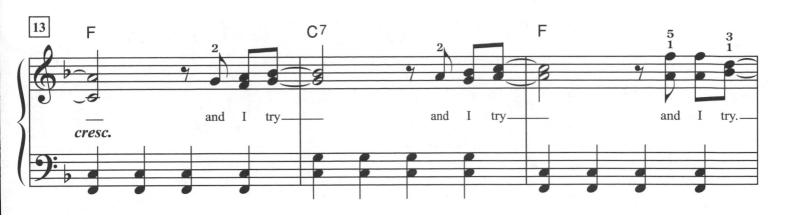

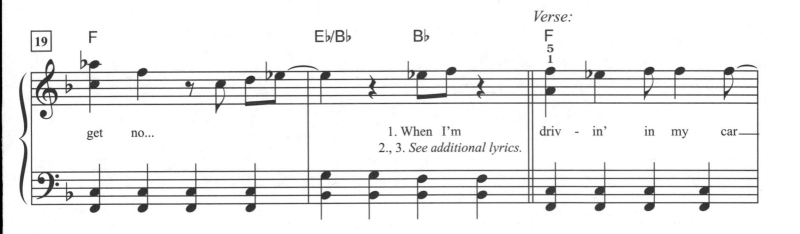

tell - in' me more and more___ a - bout some___ use - less in - for - ma-

- tion sup - posed to fire my im - ag - i - na - tion. I can't

get no... Oh, no, no, no.

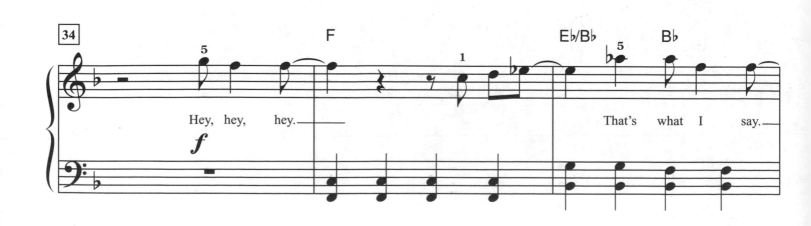

Hey, hey, hey.___ That's what I say.

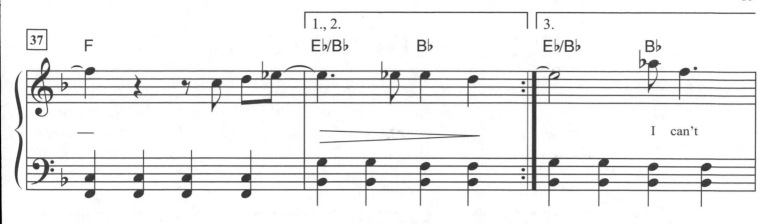

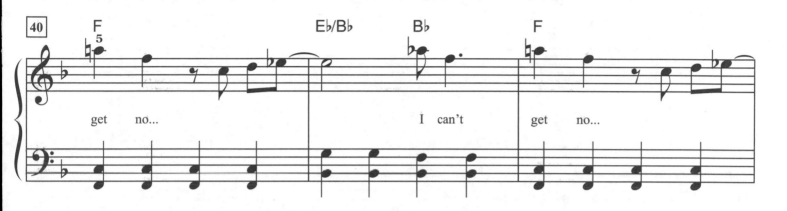

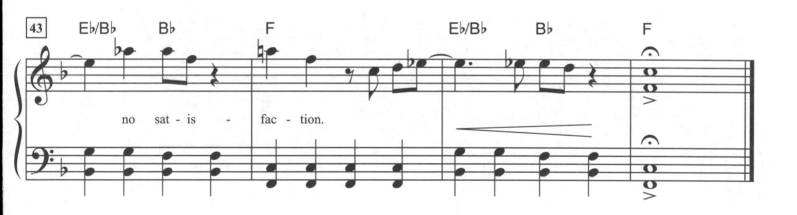

Verse 2:
When I'm watchin' my T.V.
And a man comes on and tells me
How white my shirts can be.
But, he can't be a man
'Cause he doesn't smoke the same cigarettes as me.
I can't get no,
Oh, no, no, no.

Verse 3:
When I'm ridin' 'round the world,
And I'm doin' this and I'm signin' that,
And I'm tryin' to make some girl,
Who tells me, baby, better come back maybe next week.
'Cause you see I'm on a losin' streak.
I can't get no,
Oh, no, no, no.

SWEET CHILD O' MINE

Words and Music by Steven Adler, Saul Hudson,
Duff Mckagan, W. Axl Rose and Izzy Stradlin
Arranged by Dan Coates

-'ry-thing was as fresh as the bright blue sky.

Now and then, when I see her face, she

takes me a-way to that spe-cial place, and if I stare too long, I'd

pro-'bly break down and cry.

Chorus:

Whoa, whoa,—— whoa, sweet child o' mine.——

Whoa, oh, oh, oh,——— sweet love o' mine.

Whoa, whoa,—— whoa, sweet child o' mine.

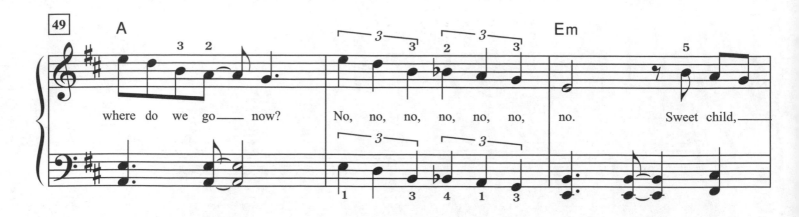

where do we go——now? No, no, no, no, no, no, no. Sweet child,——

—— sweet child—————————————————————————— o'

rit. e dim.

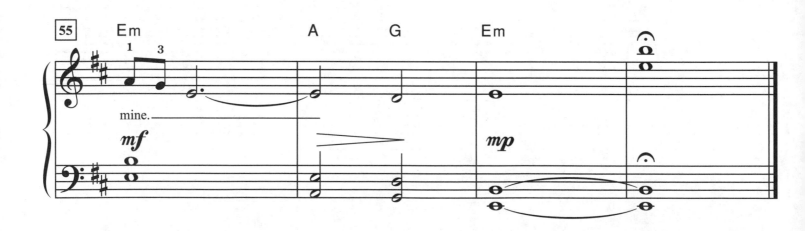

mine.————————————————

mf

mp

Verse 2:
She's got eyes of the bluest skies,
As if they thought of rain.
I hate to look into those eyes and see
An ounce of pain.
Her hair reminds me of a warm safe place
Where as a child I'd hide
And pray for the thunder and the rain to quietly
Pass me by.
(To Chorus:)

THUNDER ROAD

Words and Music by Bruce Springsteen
Arranged by Dan Coates

TINY DANCER

Words and Music by
Elton John and Bernie Taupin
Arranged by Dan Coates

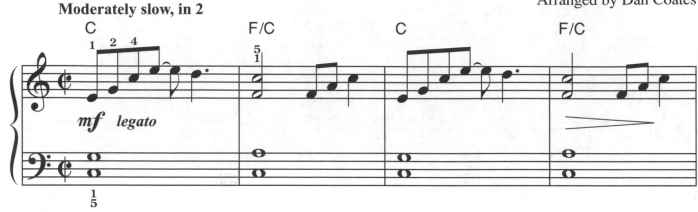

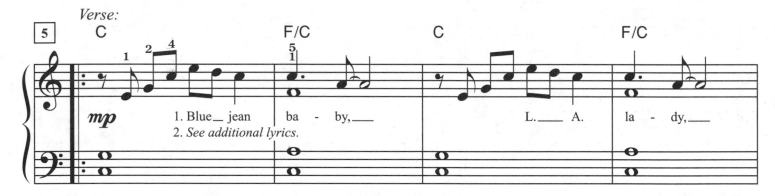

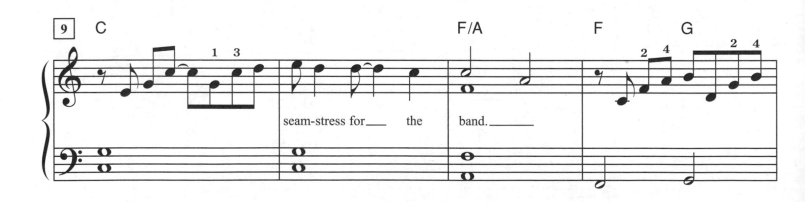

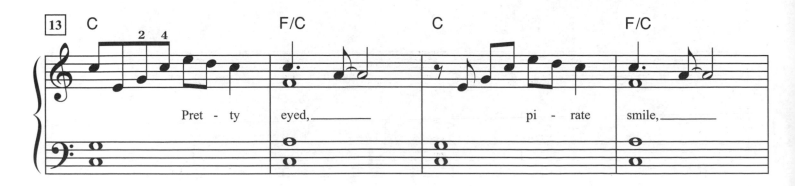

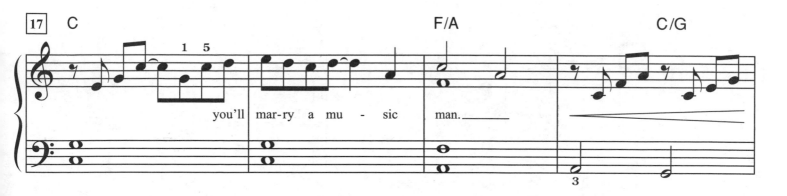

you'll mar-ry a mu - sic man.___

Bal-le - ri - na, you must__ have seen__ her,

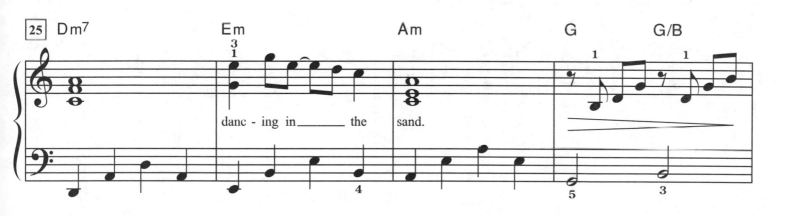

danc - ing in_____ the sand.

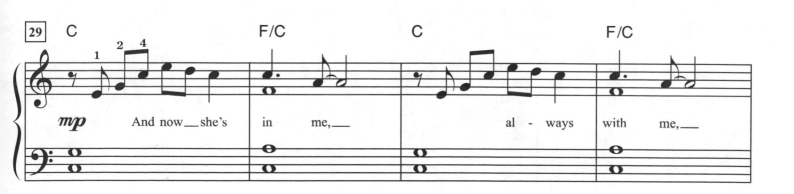

mp And now__she's in me,___ al - ways with me,___

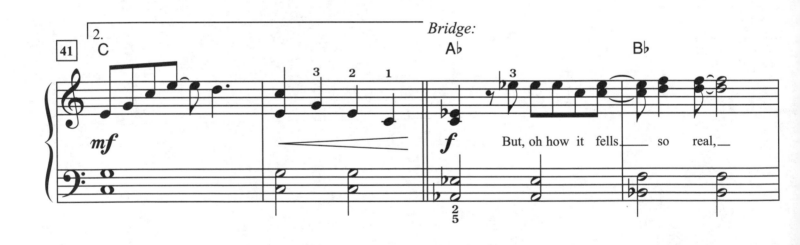

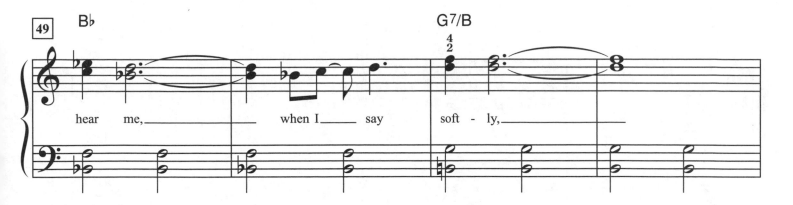

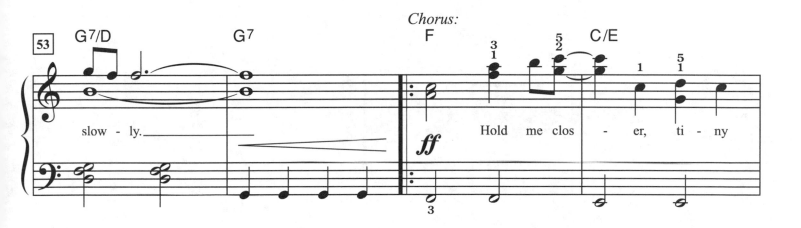

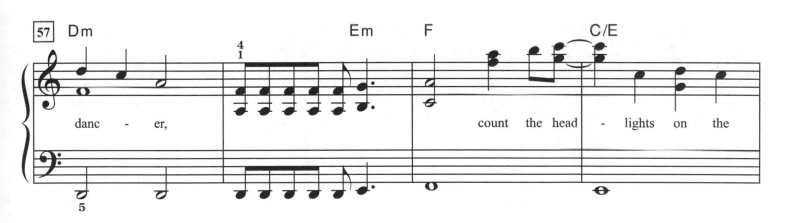

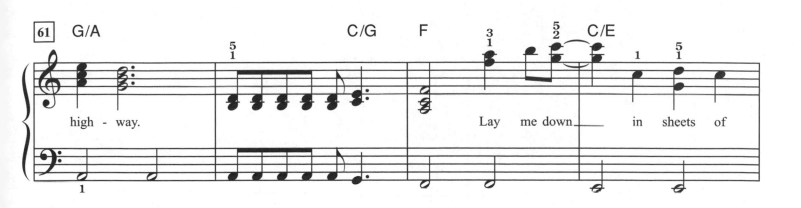

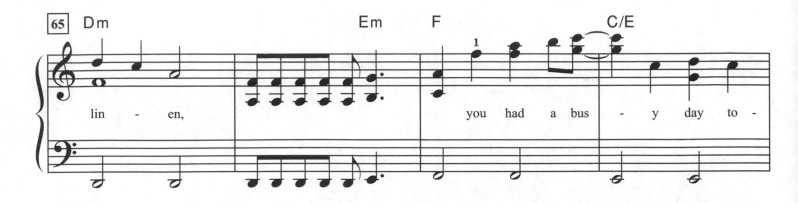

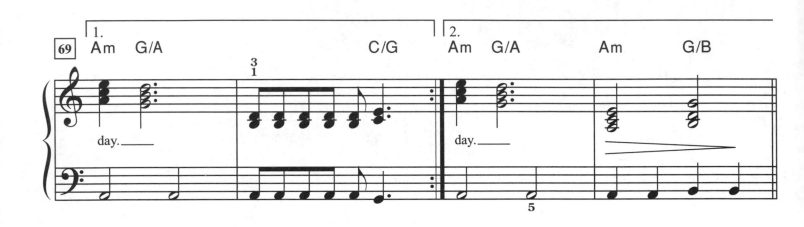

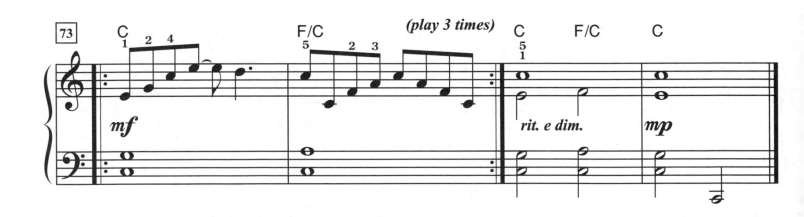

Verse 2:
Jesus freaks out in the street
Handing ticket out for God.
Turning back, she just laughs.
The boulevard is not that bad.
Piano man, he makes a stand
In the auditorium.
Looking on, she sings the songs.
The words she knows,
The tune she hums.
(To Bridge and Chorus:)

THE WEIGHT

Words and Music by Robbie Robertson
Arranged by Dan Coates

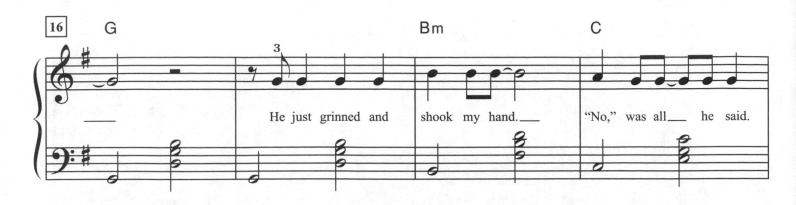

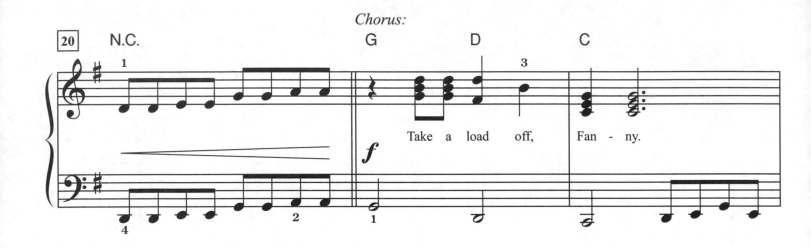

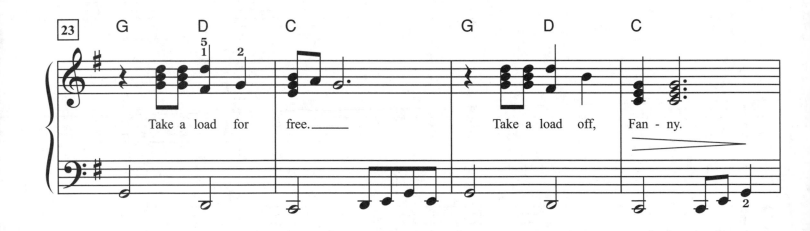

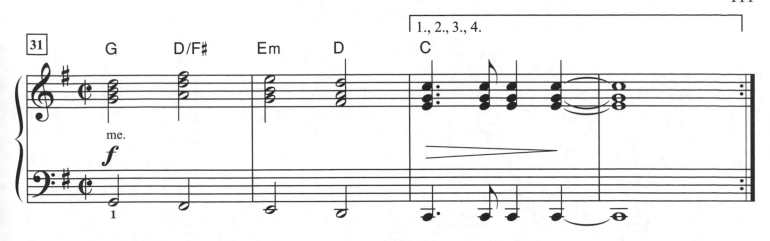

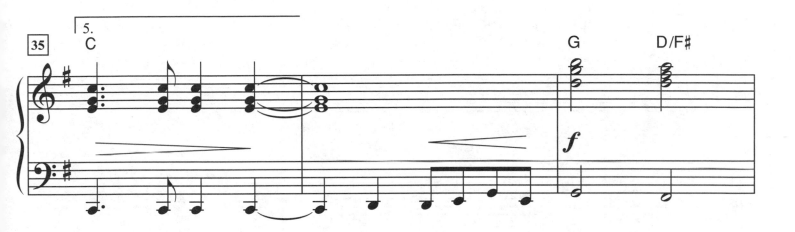

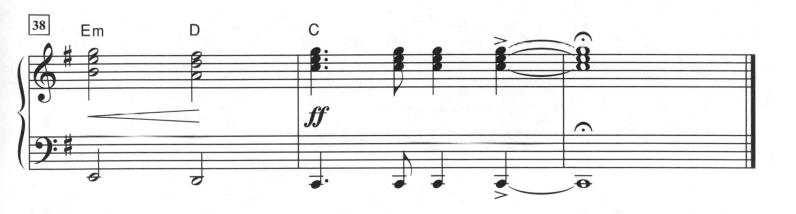

Verse 2:
I picked up my bag, I went lookin' for a place to hide,
When I saw Carmen and the devil walkin' side by side.
I said, "Hey, Carmen, come on, let's go downtown."
He said, "I gotta go, but my friend can stick around."
(To Chorus:)

Verse 3:
Go down, Miss Moses, there's nothing that you can say.
It's just old Luke, and Luke's waitin' on the Judgement Day.
I said, "Luke, my friend, what about young Anna Lee?"
He said, "Do me a favor, son,
Won't you stay and keep Anna Lee company."
(To Chorus:)

Verse 4:
Crazy Chester followed me and he caught me in the fog.
He said, "I'll fix your rack if you'll take Jack, my dog."
I said, "Wait a minute, Chester, you know I'm a peaceful man."
He said, "That's okay, boy, won't you feed him when you can."
(To Chorus:)

Verse 5:
Catch a cannonball, now take me down the line.
My bag is sinkin' low and I do believe it's time
To get back to Miss Fanny,
You know she's the only one
Who sent me here with her regards for everyone.
(To Chorus:)

WHAT'D I SAY

Words and Music by Ray Charles
Arranged by Dan Coates

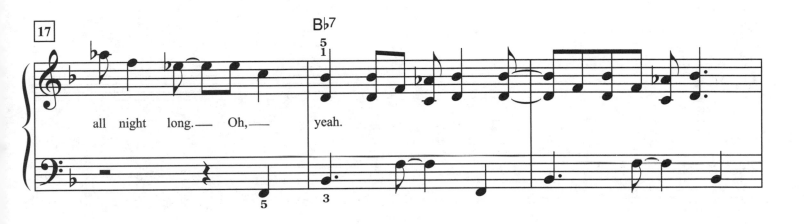

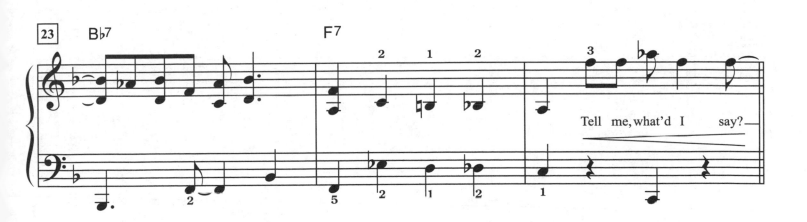

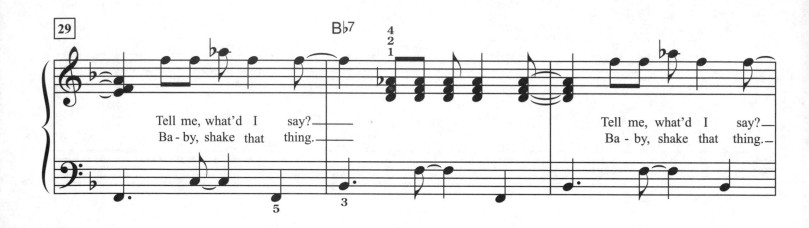

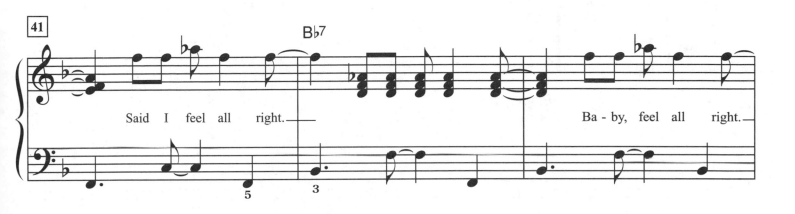

YOU SEND ME

Words and Music by Sam Cooke
Arranged by Dan Coates

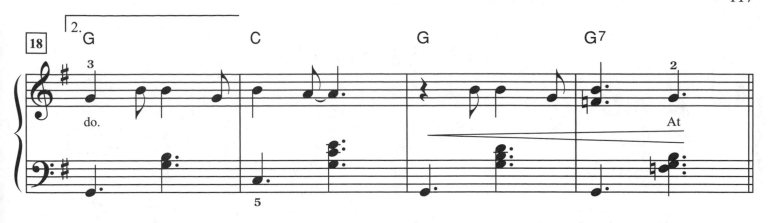

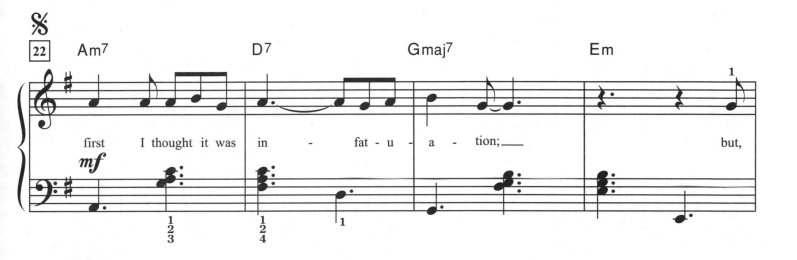

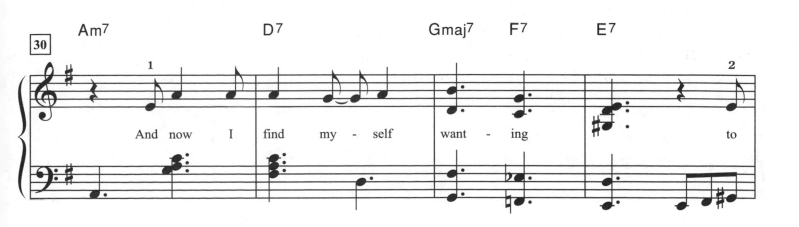